ANDY RITCHIE
THE PRICE OF VICE

ANDY RITCHIE
THE PRICE OF VICE

With thanks to my sons Mark and Stephen, my mother and my family.

Brief extracts of this book first appeared in *Flawed Genius; Scottish Football's Self-Destructive Mavericks* by Stephen McGowan (Birlinn 2009) and are reproduced with the kind permission of Birlinn, with grateful thanks.

Pictures are reproduced with the kind permission of the *Greenock Telegraph*.

First published in Great Britain in 2012 by The Derby Books Publishing Company Limited, 3 The Parker Centre, Derby, DE21 4SZ.

ISBN 978-1-78091-011-6

Printed and bound by Gomer, Llandysul Ceredigion.

Contents

Prologue

14 May 1972

JOCK STEIN smiled blandly and said: 'I think we should take stock. Now, what did we do?

'We won the League Championship. We won the Scottish Cup, we were runners-up in the League Cup and we were not beaten in any of our European matches. I would say we did alright.'

And he spread his hands and looked round for confirmation.

He was having a bit of fun rubbing in, once again, the considerable achievements of his Celtic team and piling on the discomfort for those who had been sceptical about his ability to change the team and still keep winning.

When Stein had had his fun he said: 'That's the past, it's all history now and who wants to know about that? Come and look at the future.'

He took us out to the field where there was a practice match between two teams of 14-16-year-olds.

The football was shattering in that it was so fast and skilful and pure and devoid of the physical. One might have been in Brazil.

As I remember this used to be the age group where boys were leggy and gauche, but these teams moved as thoroughbreds. Where such boys used to chase the ball these were organised and the covering in defence and the use of the space were of the best professional quality.

They produced the big wide grin on Stein's face that denotes ecstasy and only really good football tends to send him into such raptures.

He nudged me; 'what do you think of that left-back?'

I told him, 'leave me alone, I want to watch that centre-forward.'

He was a big fellow called Ritchie who is on the ground staff. He is 15 and stands an impressive 6ft 1in. Already at this age he is John Charles, gentle in his play, accurate and creative in his passing and on the run his great stride devours ground.

He has other little embellishments such as accurate heading and he knocked a cross ball six yards with his chest to make a chance for another. All these players are being brought up to appreciate that the skills are all-important and without them there is no place for anyone at the club.

Of that Stein said: 'We have the satisfaction that we are doing something useful for the game in general.'

John Rafferty
The Observer

Chapter One

The Price of Vice

A MAN knows the time is passing when regrets take the place of his dreams. For me that happened somewhere around my 28th birthday.

I was born on 23 February 1956 in Bellshill Maternity Hospital, Lanarkshire. But by the age of 27 I had dumped my boots in a bin full of greyhound shit. I had chased my last hare.

I'll be blunt. My career and my life, compared to the rich promise of my early Celtic years under Jock Stein, have been a major let down, a cursed disappointment. Not only to me, but to many others as well.

By allowing my career to end so soon I failed my family, especially my two sons Mark and Stephen. I was never living the life of a professional athlete, never leading by example.

I knew two years after I finished playing – sometime around 1985 – and had gone to London to work as assistant secretary in the Barbican Centre what I had done. It was office and leisure work, a good steady job with a solid income and nothing to do with football. Boredom was not quite a statutory condition of employment, but it could never match the thrill of scoring goals.

And I woke one morning with an aching realisation. I was sweating and suffering one of my increasingly familiar panic attacks.

The game was up; I could not do it anymore. I would never kick a ball as a professional again. I was playing amateur football on a Sunday morning and, unaware of my former life, a Leyton Orient scout asked me along for a trial. I refused. I had fallen out of love with a game I had briefly excelled in.

I was bad enough being left to my own devices for six weeks in the close season. Back then I only had to look at a pie and a pint and I would pile on six pounds.

Now, here I was in an office job, enjoying my life to the full. And as my life was filling out so was my waistline. I was a young man with responsibilities. And I woke up that day and said to myself, 'that's it, I'll never play football again'.

Before he died in 1996 my father, Andrew senior, said often that I could have done more in the game. Even when the sun gods were smiling on my career at Parkhead and Morton.

In my younger days he would come home from watching the game I had featured in and the conversation would always go the same way.

'How did he do today dad?' my mother would ask.

'Ach,' came the standard reply, 'he never moved about and he was hopeless.'

Mother would come back with, 'aye, but how many did he score?'

And with a scowl my dad would say, 'just the two'.

'Just the two?' she would exclaim, 'he must have done something right'.

'Aye,' replied my old man, 'but he could have done mair.'

And that was that. My dad was a man of few words, but he had a talent for nailing the truth to the wall with one line.

Close my eyes and I can still paint a picture of the day I was crowned Scotland's Player of the Year. Season 1978–79 was drawing to a close and I was the top scorer in the Premier League with 22 League goals for Morton. I had topped Celtic's Frank McGarvey, Rangers stand out Gordon Smith and Joe Harper of Aberdeen in the scoring charts.

A part-time player, I supported my family by working in sales for Dunne & Moore, the soft drinks firm once based a stone's throw from Celtic Park, where I started out. I was also doing some delivery work for a meat packaging company.

I was a married man of 22 with a young son and as the warmer days of May came around we needed a little extra money for a family holiday. That was despite my burgeoning income from celebrity endorsements and appearances. So I took a weekend job laying tar on the roads.

Which explains why, on the day I was recognised by Scotland's sports writers, I was digging trenches in Bothwell.

Teammates and friends passed in taxis en route to an early warm-up session for the main event. At one point Johnny Marr and Bobby Houston of Partick Thistle gazed down on me as I wiped sweat from my soaking brow.

This was a different era, far removed from the riches of today's pampered millionaires. It would be hard to imagine a Rangers captain or Celtic's Scott Brown preparing to accept a glittering award by putting in a shift on the roads.

Here I was at my peak, the so-called Idle Idol. I parked my car outside a primary school in Greenock one day and young boys were playing football in the playground. One of the lads scored a screamer past the obligatory fat kid in goal. And as I turned the lock in my car door I heard the shout; 'AND RITCHIE SCORES'. I thought he was taking the piss. He was not; the kid had not even seen me. At that time my reputation for spectacular goals and stunning free-kicks was growing all around the country. I was being recognised in the unlikeliest places, from Laurencekirk to Lochee.

I had plenty of good times and I enjoyed them to the full. I made my Celtic debut at 17. I started 247 games in Morton's first team and scored 129 goals, a record of a goal every two games. I finished the top scorer in the Scottish Premier League. I won the Scottish Football Writers' player of the year. And I had come close to the World Cup squad in Argentina the year before until the Scottish Football Association, in their infinite wisdom, decided a part-time player was unfit for purpose.

But by 1983 I was close to being out of the game. The best I could do by the time I finished was a game for Albion Rovers, where I briefly managed, and a trial for Stranraer.

Why was that? I ask myself the same question every second day and come up with the same observations.

In my own head all was not well. I was a sick young man.

Explaining why is no easy task; let us just say I have always had what you might describe as an addictive personality.

Drink, soft drugs, gambling, depression; I have done each and every one of those to excess. I was no role model for the kids in Greenock, Glasgow's east end or anywhere else for that matter.

It would be easy to blame others for my demise. But when the buck stops, a mirror is sufficient to identify the true arbiter of my downfall.

In November 2006 my life was scarred by career malfunction, marital breakdown and family strife. My mental health was poor and I suffered a nervous breakdown. For a time I moved from sofa to sofa, taking advantage of the kindness of friends and family.

At the invitation of the Scottish Professional Footballers' Association I was guided towards residential help.

I needed help and a roof over my head. Three decades after being the best player in the country I was effectively homeless.

These days things are better and I do not wake up every morning with regrets anymore; only every second day. Bit by bit I am rebuilding my life.

On reflection I did not handle it all properly. I socialised, I partied, I had a good crack at the whip. Too much for my own good. I have had a lot of happy days and more than a few boozy nights, but in the context of football this much is clear.

I not only cheated myself, I also cheated a lot of other good people as well.

I drank too much, I smoked too much and unlike Bill Clinton, I did inhale when the marijuana joints were being passed around. It would not be uncommon for me to be blind drunk on a Friday night before a game against Rangers or Celtic, nursing a raging hangover as kick-off approached. As a young Celtic player I was better, but the signs were always there.

I cheated big Jock Stein in my days there and he knew I was cheating him. The most successful manager in Celtic's history, that man was nobody's mug. He had witnessed the likes of me come and go, having so much to offer and failing to do so for whatever reason.

'Aaaach,' was his usual way of ending a conversation with me. He threw his arms up in the air in a fit of exasperation the day I turned down a four-year contract, prompting him to sell me to Morton. John Clark, the Lisbon Lions defender and one of the loveliest men you will meet, also came in to do some work with the young players at Celtic at that time and he must have been horrendously frustrated with me as well.

They told me that at the time, but I had stopped listening. Or if I did listen, I could not take it in.

I am not offering up any excuses. I never did before and I will not start now. But let me put it like this; I always had my demons to conquer. And more often than not the demons won by a knockout.

I have not lived my whole life with a big dark cloud hanging over me. Christ, I like a laugh. I have always been known as that great Scottish catch-all phrase, 'a character'.

But there have been periods, dark, prolonged periods, of my life where I have suffered from depression. And those closest to me, suffered involuntarily by my side. My life has always been akin to the big dipper at Blackpool Pleasure Beach. I have been up and I have been down.

I suffered the panic attacks regularly and have done for most of my adult life. In good times and in bad.

I suffered badly during my Player of the Year season. Here I was in my heyday, big ambling Andy, tearing up the Premier League and the poster boy of every kid with a dad in the shipyards, a rare shaft of light in a gloomy, post-industrial landscape.

But no one had the slightest concept of what was really swimming around this head of mine. I may have shone light into the lives of others, but I was casting my own prospects into a shaft beyond the reach of the great cranes, which straddled the Clyde. Mine was a head, which spent a great deal of time up its own rear end.

I kept bad time, I was cheeky, and I did not try terribly hard. We were always told at Morton to report to the Tontine Hotel in Greenock on a match day for our pre-match meal. The manager Benny Rooney would stand at the top of the steps, inside the glass-fronted door waiting for me.

Meanwhile I would be sneaking in a window at the back of the building, taking my seat and waiting for him coming back to the table where I would protest my innocence all along. He would fine me there and then. But on the Monday I would just go to the legendary chairman Hal Stewart and threaten to leave if there was a penny missing from my wages the next week.

I played the emotional blackmail card to shameless perfection. Hal thought of me as one of his own, an extension to his family. Albeit an offspring he hoped he might sell for £1 million for one day. His paternalism was always laced with a hint of self-interest.

People just thought this kind of behaviour was part of the Andy Ritchie facade. Big Andy, they would say, sets the world alight, but does not bother his arse with authority. A rebel without a clue.

And sometimes I would be less than honest. I would let them think they were right. The truth is that it annoyed me when I heard all that shit because it was inaccurate. Looking back now I did all that stuff because I had problems.

I was covering up the inconvenient truth; the reality of my life I did not want the outside world to see. They were welcome to the extravagant goals, the free-kicks, the bending corners, the flicks, the feints, the toothy grin. But they never got to see me, the man behind the image. They just thought they did.

Andy does not give a fuck, they would say, he just walks out on things because he does not care about authority.

What they did not know was that when Andy was dying inside with depression or a panic attack or a hangover, that is when he did not hang about.

When I feel as if I am going to die sitting in front of you I will not lie down and succumb, I'll get the hell out of there thanks.

If I felt a panic attack coming on in a team meeting or on a foreign trip I would just get up and walk out. Just like that. Not a word of explanation, nothing.

The football generally took care of itself so it probably only happened two or three times. But when it did I would head for the toilet where I would have a stash of cigarettes and matches wrapped up in foil on the ledge over the cistern. And I would have a fag in the toilet while I calmed down.

I would feel I could not breathe, place my hands on the walls to stop them closing in and, being the son of a working class man from Lanarkshire, I had no desire to let people see that.

The heavy breathing, the sweats, I can feel them now. I still do from time to time. The symptoms come sober or drunk, they do not care to discriminate.

If anything the excessive drinking made the panic attacks worse, it brought them on with a vengeance. How could it be otherwise?

I would be waking up on the morning of a game at my peak unable to remember where I had left my car. I would lose my wallet, wonder where I was.

It mattered little who we were playing, it could have been Celtic, Rangers or Alloa Athletic.

I would panic, thinking 'how am I going to get to Greenock for kick-off?' I would phone one or two of the boys and they would take me to the car park of the Windmill Tavern in Uddingston where the car had usually been left after a session the night before. I would be a worried man and I had been sweating. And I had to have a drink to sort that out. Pronto.

All the while I was behaving like that I was perpetuating the core problem, I was adding to my tales of woe.

But when I was at the peak of my career you got on with it. Drink? Depression? Panic attacks? Do not be ridiculous, son, get your boots on, roll up your sleeves and get out there. Walking into Jock Stein or Jock Wallace's office at Motherwell and declaring myself unfit to play because of a bout of depression was never an option.

You avoid exposing yourself in the West of Scotland. If you are conscious of your acne in this part of the world you do not smile and folk think you are a dour faced bastard. They do not ask questions, they judge first.

If you cannot read you steer clear of signs. What you do not do – and thankfully this is less the case than it once was thanks to bodies like the PFA Scotland – is own up and seek help. I wish to God I could have.

In my day you looked for strategies to avoid putting yourself in the situations you dreaded. If there's a sand bank you bury yourself neck deep.

This, then, is my public therapy. My attempt to explain, to apologise where appropriate and to tell the truth, the whole truth and nothing but the truth through the eyes of Andy Ritchie. There will be times in the telling of my story when I will paint myself in an unfavourable light. So be it.

I have read footballers' memoirs where the players cover themselves in two coats of white paint for public consumption then pick up the cheque. That is not me.

My old friend Frank McGarvey told his tale with commendable honesty, lifting the lid on his gambling addiction.

It was no surprise to me; I attended Gambler's Anonymous meetings for five years and every three weeks Frankie would be sitting by my side. It would be fair to say that neither of us ever bought into what we were being told 100%.

I always stood accused of failing to put my all into running about a football park. But when it comes to boozing and betting on horses, football and greyhounds I have never been anything other than industrious.

And that has taken its toll as well. On family, on friends, on my relationships. You would have to ask my wife if that finished my marriage but let me put it this way; it did not help.

How could it when I lost family homes through gambling? And cars?

I had that spell where I went for some help for it. So much so that I did not gamble a penny for five years. But that was then.

The urge to gamble still eats away at me. Any addiction is a constant problem and I fight it every single day.

Some days I win the fight but Mr Bookmaker wins on others by a clear majority. Most of them in fact – even when I think I have won. The men in the camel coats always have the last laugh – they know I will be back.

One day I will win and they will have no comeback. But only when I am not here any longer; if you are not on this earth you do not punt or drink to excess. I have never been an alcoholic, but I have always drunk to excess.

I look now at guys like Paul Gascoigne with that poor lad's litany of problems and it occurs to me that they are right when they say there is only a hair's breadth between genius and madness.

I cannot relate to most of these guys like Gazza too much because they made millions of pounds from football.

I have never been a millionaire and I never will be. The best money I ever made as a footballer was £200 a week at Morton. That was a good wage then, but the guys on the North Sea oilrigs were earning more then than the best player in Scotland. I dread to think what might have happened to my life had I enjoyed the riches of the average Celtic or Rangers player now. Chances are I would be dead.

As things stand I remain one of life's survivors. And minus the gloss, the emulsion or the wallpaper of so many footballing memoirs this is the rise and fall of Andy Ritchie.

Chapter Two

A Futile Feud

TOMMY BURNS was a man who deserved to scratch an old head.

The impish, fair-haired boy who brushed the Parkhead terraces died a man of 51. No one who lived as exemplary a life as Thomas – as I knew him all my days – deserves that.

From the day we met as teenagers to the day he died I regarded Tommy as a friend at heart. But we disagreed a hell of a lot. Right till the end when I stubbornly refused to patch up our final feud prior to his death. It is difficult to express how much I regret that now.

It matters little how the final chasm between us took root and lingered. Suffice to say, we had both helped someone who betrayed us very badly and Tommy was more forgiving than me. It was as serious a matter as we had ever fallen out over, something so hurtful that it can bring me to the brink of tears even now. And yet in light of Tommy's death it suddenly does not seem so important.

I remember when the row came to a head in the summer of 2004, when we ended up arguing in the Hampden car park. We met in a car in the far corner of this great open space and as the accusations flew – all from my direction I should add – I cried tears of anger. Thomas was deeply, deeply hurt for me and for all the things, which had brought this matter to a head.

When you are hurting and nursing a grievance you do not take it out on the man in the street. You turn on those closest to you; I said some stupid things. Tommy did not answer me, possibly because there was nothing he could say.

I became angrier and angrier and as I did so he threw his head back. We had wasted so much time protecting a football person who had betrayed us both so badly and the repercussions of that will plague me until the day I die.

I do not know what I wanted Tommy to say in response. All I know is that I needed him to say something, which would somehow alleviate my pain. I was being deeply selfish and I can see that now. I was also being unreasonable because there was nothing Thomas could say that could make things better.

That night did not end relations completely. But from then on there was always something between us, always a distance which never existed in our days as skinny kids finding our way on the Celtic ground staff.

I would call up for tickets for games and we would chat away, but it was not the same. At the Scottish Football Writers' Dinner in 2007 Tommy attended in his role as first team coach under Gordon Strachan. And we stood on the steps of the Thistle Hotel in Glasgow's Cambridge Street where the arguing started up once more.

I got angry with him and he responded because he knew there was nothing he could say to make things better.

Our bonds had always run deep, even outwith our time as Quality Street Kids at Parkhead. My wife Rena had known Tommy from the age of 14 and his wife Rosemary got to know Rena and Frank McGarvey's wife Pauline from going to a help group for the wives of compulsive gamblers. They were a friendly band – though unlike Frank and me Tommy was never a betting man.

The first I heard of his illness was when a journalist called to ask me if I had heard anything. I thought it was the kind of story in which Glasgow specialises; an urban myth.

I am ashamed to say that my initial thought was a horrible misapprehension. 'He'll be alright,' I thought, 'it's only skin cancer.' Only skin cancer, I said blithely. 'He'll stay out the sun, wear a hat and he'll be fine.'

When I spoke to Rena about it she confirmed she had been speaking to Tommy's wife Rosemary. They had not wanted to tell me the news for fear of upsetting me; which served only to upset me more. How could they keep this from me?

I phoned my buddy, the ex-Partick Thistle manager Gerry Collins. Gerry was also a great friend of Tommy's and the best man at his wedding. Incredibly he knew nothing either.

I felt like the Grim Reaper passing on news like that. If I cannot get a laugh out of something I am struggling; I keep it to myself. Gerry could not get his head around the fact that journalists seemed to know the news before us, his oldest friends. In my case it was maybe a sign of how far I had allowed our friendship to drift.

Gerry called Tommy and confirmed the news by phone. I could never have done that with Thomas. I cannot say why; it was just the case that we would never have got there. He did not like to talk about anything bad concerning himself; he would rather talk about you or your problems for 45 minutes.

As kids at Celtic I would tell him he was in the wrong profession; he should have been a priest. I am not a catholic, but Tommy would effectively take my confession every second day when we were 17.

He would suck in his lips at the appropriate point of a story, shut his eyes and make all the right noises. He was a natural, sympathetic and willing listener. But ask him to talk about himself and it was a different story. Silence, change the subject; every tactic in the book.

We had battled out plenty of rows over the years. I remember Rena telling me one day that there was a job on the go at Celtic Park in the early to mid 1990s. Big Jim McCafferty had lost the kit man's job and Rena came off the phone to order me to call Thomas Burns. I needed work and Rosemary had told her there was a job at Parkhead.

It was a steady post with a steady income and at the time I needed that. What is more, it was a job for life.

I called Tommy straight away and his response was disparaging.

'You're kidding me on,' he said, 'that's a job for an old man.'

'Have you looked at me lately?' I fired back, ignoring the fact I was not yet 40. 'I need a job. I know that job; I've watched it being done since I was 14. It's travel all over Europe, the best of hotels and one of the biggest clubs in the world. And I'd get paid for it – every month. I need a steady wage.'

Thomas pondered this then snapped; 'alright, come in and see me tomorrow morning and we will get it sorted out.'

I went in on the Sunday morning and he and Billy Stark, his assistant, were standing there. Tommy looked at me blankly; he had forgotten I was coming. This, I should add, was normal behaviour from Thomas.

When I reminded him he went away to discuss it with Starky. By the time he died in May 2008 we still had not finished the conversation. He had obviously encountered some opposition to the idea and he could not bring himself to let down one of his oldest pals.

The only time I ever brought it up was in anger many years later.

'You love to give out good news,' I told him. 'But you left me sitting in a chair for two and a half hours that Sunday morning rather than telling me you'd had a rethink and letting me down gently. After all the years I've known you.'

It was typical of the kind of row we would have, but it was harsh. Tommy did take me back to Celtic as a youth coach then a scout and they were some of the best years of my life.

All through our years as colleagues and pals Tommy did not like the way I behaved, the way I drank, the way I spoke. He was wrong a lot of the time, I was wrong the others.

That's friendship; true friends bicker and fall out. But deep down they are still friends.

I finally saw Tommy after the news of the cancer at Easter Road, the home of Hibs, when I was on duty as an SPL delegate for Celtic's visit.

Any awkwardness was blown away by his usual response.

'TRUMPTON!' he roared, using the nickname I had acquired years before due to my alleged resemblance to the cartoon bear that used to appear on telly in the mornings. At Morton I changed from being Trumpton the Bear to Baloo the Bear after the Jungle Book.

But to Tommy I was always Trumpton and that day we shared a hug. No words were necessary. By now he had been to London to have the illness diagnosed fully. When I next spoke to him we finally discussed the 'C' word – we were edging our way around it slowly – and he was typically upbeat.

'It's alright big man,' said Thomas. 'I'm getting treatment, I'll be fine.' And that was that. Welcome to the world of the West of Scotland male.

I did not really understand his disease. I thought skin cancer was a mole you cut out. It did not get to your lungs, it did not tear through your bones; you cut it out and you wore a hat in the sun. How wrong can you be?

It will always be a deep regret of mine that I was not there for Thomas, that I allowed my own self-absorption to ride above his needs.

By the time the cancer was too far gone, by the time people close to both of us were telling us he was dying, it was too late.

I had said so much to the man, too much, and I was deeply embarrassed. I could not handle serious conversations at the best of times so how could I go to a man I loved as a friend and say, 'sorry I said all that now you're dying.' It would have been crass in the extreme.

The last time I spoke to Thomas was at Love Street, Paisley on Sunday 24 February 2008. I'll always have that date in my mind now. I was the SPL's official observer for Celtic's visit to St Mirren, a part-time role, which made me a kind of arbitrator and League representative.

I had to make sure everything was in place and before the game I saw Thomas in the middle of the park warming up with the team and juggling a ball.

I shouted to him from the sidelines; 'Aye, the old skills are still the best partner.'

Thomas beckoned me onto the pitch and we hugged. We asked after each other and our families and exchanged small talk, then he told me to come up for a cup of tea after the game, but it was my impression – possibly wrongly – that he could not get away from me quick enough. I could not say by then that I blamed him.

As events turned out, Shunsuke Nakamura – Celtic's Japanese midfielder – scored a highly controversial free-kick which left St Mirren bitterly unhappy. The manager Gus McPherson was an angry man and perhaps because of that the Celtic coaching staff did not come upstairs for a cuppa. The goalkeeping coach Jim Blyth nipped up and made apologies on their behalf, saying they were climbing on the bus to make a quick getaway.

I thought later about phoning Thomas at home. But I thought better of it. 'I'll see him at a game soon,' I thought. I was wrong.

Within seven weeks Thomas Burns, Celtic legend, was dead. I would never see him again.

Chapter Three

Mr Stein, Tommy B and Me

AS A KID I never thought of becoming a professional footballer, did not even give it a consideration.

A spring-like Sunday afternoon early in 1971 changed things. I had been encouraged by my father to play in a trial game arranged in Cumbernauld by Middlesbrough to seek out young Scots talent. A neighbour, Bill Adamson, who coached the Bellshill YM team where I started out, drove me along with two or three friends.

To say I was ill-prepared for what lay ahead would be putting things mildly. I had barely kicked a ball competitively in combat and was only there for a kick about.

My expectations were low – and when I lasted just 25 minutes before being hauled from the field it seemed my pessimism was well founded.

Little did I know until later that Harold Sheperdson, assistant trainer to Alf Ramsay with the England team, had taken me off quickly to stop the scouts from other clubs from noticing me. He had been too late.

Sheperdson asked me down to Ayrsome Park for further trials there and then. They would not let me leave the trial without agreeing – it was their gig after all. So I said yes.

I got outside eventually and found Celtic's scout waiting for me. Coventry City were also keen for a word and they were in the old English First Division – now known as the Premiership – at the time.

When I got clear of those two I arrived back at the house to find a Rangers scout sitting there with my mother and father, Andrew and Bessie.

I was 15 at the time. To say I was naive would be putting it mildly. But I had a fantastic childhood.

I have an older brother Liam and Jan, a sister five years younger than me. My dad worked in Rolls-Royce and my mother as a cleaner in Bellshill. There was never a massive amount of cash around, but always enough to get by. We were a normal family and I cannot point to a single thing in my childhood, which would explain any of my indiscretions thereafter. We had normal holidays in Rothesay and Saltcoats and we did what decent, respectable families did in the West of Scotland.

My father also took me to watch Motherwell when he could. When the chance suddenly came for me to be a footballer it was, then, a source of substantial excitement.

The Rangers scout had left Cumbernauld as soon as he saw the others hanging about. He got wise, found out my home address and knocked on the door.

It was February or March as I recall – but that did not stop my old man checking the calendar to make sure it was not the first of April.

The Rangers fella, I cannot remember his name now, started on the doorstep by asking my mother if her son's name was Andrew. She thought he was the police. She nearly fainted, believing I must have been run over by a bus.

But he came into the living room and he must have known already what school I went to. Rangers, at that time, deemed Catholics surplus to requirements. Bellshill Academy, where I attended, was on the approved list as it were.

It emerged after the man from Rangers had accepted our hospitality that the Celtic fella had also been in touch by telephone to say he would come round to see my parents on the Monday night. Crafty? Sly? As I would find out years later from doing the job myself you could not paint a red neck on a football scout.

Before he turned up, however, the surreal new path my life was taking took one more twist.

On the Monday afternoon, the brother-in-law of Manchester United manager Matt Busby, Jimmy Mathie, arrived on my mother's doorstep. This was becoming ridiculous. But exhilarating at the same time.

At the age of 15, Celtic, Rangers and Manchester United were all after me for Christ's sake. In time Chelsea and West Brom would also invite me south for trials. To begin with I went down to Manchester for a few days and soaked up the Old Trafford atmosphere. But Middlesbrough had got to me first and, true to my first promise to Harold Sheperdson I spent quite a bit of time travelling down with Tony McAndrew, another Scot who ended up playing there for 10 years.

In those days you signed what was called an S-Form, a kind of tie up with a senior club to go onto their staff – but before you did it you kept them dangling a bit.

Schoolwork? That was shunted to the side, who needed it?

I was never the greatest at school anyway. I did better the year Craig Brown, the former Scotland manager, was my headmaster.

I liked to play with the school team and he took my final year at Belvidere Primary before going off to play with the big boys. It was Craig's first posting after giving up football, where he played for Rangers and Dundee, and completing his teacher training.

He was an encouraging figure to me because he took the school team.

We knew he had enjoyed a decent career as a professional and at that age you tend to take a bit more notice of people like that than you do someone's dad for example. I actually won prizes at school the year Craig was my teacher.

When I left high school with little to distinguish me academically I did take a job as an apprentice with an engineering company, but that did not last long.

Celtic offered me a ground staff position. And they were my preferred option because they had the best players – it was that simple.

I had been training at Celtic on a Tuesday night and Ibrox at the Albion Training Ground on a Thursday. And being so close to my folks had its advantages.

For me there was no preference between the Old Firm clubs. I was a Motherwell supporter and all I had really wanted was for my boyhood team to take an interest.

Here I was with three or four massive clubs at the height of European football in the early 1970s after me and I would have rejected every one of them to sign up at Fir Park.

They did invite me in eventually and I met up with Bobby Howatt, who was manager at the time. But Howatt told me bluntly he had nothing for me. They had no youth team and the best he could do was offer to keep an eye on me. A let down? You'd better believe it.

I ended that season with Bellshill YM then settled on going to Celtic Boys' Club and onto the Celtic ground staff.

The day I arrived with my father to sign forms we walked in the old front door, with the stain glass Celtic sign above, just as Jackie McNamara senior was leaving. Jackie, a great human being as I would later discover, would distinguish himself with Celtic and Hibs before becoming a leading light in the player's union. He would also become father to some fine boys, one of whom – Jackie junior – was signed for Celtic by Tommy Burns many years later.

Jackie was a couple of years older than me, but as he left Jock Stein's assistant manager Sean Fallon met my father and I on the doorstep.

In his rich Irish brogue Sean ushered us in and greeted my father warmly.

'Did you have a long way to come to get here?' he asked.

'No,' said my dad, 'we took the bus from Bellshill.'

'Ah well, maybe this will cover your time and expenses,' replied Sean, peeling a crisp £50 note from a thick bundle he had just removed from his pocket.

In the early 1970s this was serious, serious money. I doubt my father had ever seen a note that big before. My decision had already been made to join Celtic, the gesture was unnecessary. But you remember these things just the same.

There were five of us taken on at that time, young boys with sky-high dreams.

The late Brian McLaughlin was the finest 16-year-old prospect I have ever seen.

He had everything, the lot. He had pace, skill, he could header the ball, he could use his left foot and his right foot and he was the closest player I have seen to Lubomir Moravcik, the Celtic great.

I first met him when he was 17 and it was clear there was a massive career waiting for him. I remember we went with Scotland's youth team to Las Palmas for a world championship tournament.

It was an Under-17 tournament and Brian won player of the tournament. This when guys like Gunter Netzer were playing for West Germany. These were the cream of the young crop from the best nations in the world. McLaughlin? He was the best player there. Bar none.

He was so head and shoulders above everyone else that he came back to go straight into Celtic's first team.

He could have been anything but for the day Willie McVeigh of Motherwell did him with a horrendous tackle; an absolutely shocking tackle. He should have been banned sine die for what he did to Brian that day. He went right over the top and I saw it clearly from my vantage point behind the dugout. I was on the Celtic ground staff at the time.

Brian had an injury, which equated to that suffered by Ian Durrant of Rangers 20 years later. Medical advances meant Durrant managed to get back and play at a reasonable level, but operations were not at that level back then.

It's fair to say Brian did not cope well with the trauma of having his career placed on the line. Understandably so. It was all about trying to get back and trying to achieve something. Trying to stop the knee beating him.

Eventually Brian did come back to become the Scottish First Division's player of the year at Ayr United. All that with one leg. So good was that leg that the other could have been wooden and he would still have been an outstanding footballer.

Ally McLeod paid £100,000 to take him back to the Scottish Premier League and he was a good player. All with one leg as stiff as a board. That's how good he was and he knew himself he was a phenomenal talent.

People said he was better than Kenny Dalglish and I would not disagree. Obviously Kenny went on to become the best player this country produced in the modern era. But Brian had the capabilities to be that man until the fates prevailed.

He was playing in the Celtic first team at 17 while Dalglish never reached that level till he was 21.

Ask any of the old men who played in the Celtic first team at that time about Brian and they would all tell you the same thing. He has everything you would ever want in a football player.

You would go away with Celtic and he would just take over entire games. Celtic had the best players in the country at the time and Brian was head and shoulders above even them. A fireman's lift above everybody else around him.

When I heard he had died at the age of 54 near Falkirk in 2009 I was devastated. It was a tragic death after all he had been through.

I had never seen a better young player at the time and after years of being involved in football I have yet to see one since.

He was by no means the only talented player in the intake I joined at Celtic.

There was Rab Prentice, who could make the ball talk. Jimmy Kyles was a prolific centre-forward from Dundee, then there was me and Thomas Burns.

Tommy was a city boy from the Calton near Celtic Park, whereas I was a 'country boy' because I came from Bellshill in Lanarkshire. You do the journey in 15 minutes by car these days – back then it was another planet from the grimy streets of Glasgow's industrial east end.

If you got the red bus to Celtic Park you were country. If you got the green and yellow bus you were city. We were different characters Tommy and me, the proverbial Little and Large. Big Jock always said that if you could combine what Tommy Burns held inside with the attributes I had on the outside as a football player then you would have some player.

There was no need; at that time we almost functioned as one anyway. There was only one thing we did not do together and that was play in the same Celtic Boys' Club side. That was because he was nine months younger than me.

Like me Tommy was a cheeky, impudent boy and big Jock knew that. We shared a sense of humour; one the manager did not always appreciate.

But we came as a package and he accepted that. Where Tommy went in those days I would follow and vice versa. We used to run back to Tommy's grandmother's house in Soho Street at lunchtime.

It was a hop and a skip from Celtic Park and we would traipse in with our football kits on, sweating and hungry after running down London Road past the small dairy.

Tommy's grandfather was not in the best of health at the time, the sun was already setting for the old fella. But Tommy's mother would have a cup of tea and a jam sandwich for us all ready.

Tommy would then sit with his old granda for 20 minutes knowing fine well the old fellow's mental faculties were diminishing. He would see imaginary spiders and rats in the bed and would cry out, 'Thomas, Thomas'. And Tommy would pull back the cover, lift his old legs carefully and remove the imagined 'rat' to make his granda feel that bit better about things.

We were only 15 and if truth be told we sometimes found it funny. But it was profoundly sad as well because as an impetuous youth with your life ahead of you it never occurs to you that the old boy might not have much longer on this earth. He did not as it transpired.

Tommy would always make a joke of it. Yet when I look back now almost 40 years later I can see that was a defence mechanism. Anyone who has known a situation like that in their home will tell you that if you did not laugh you would weep.

But there was no time for self-pity with Tommy. Neither then when his grandfather was ill or years later when his own life was coming to an end.

We would run like the clappers back along London Road, back to Parkhead for 1.30 when reserve team coach Willie Fernie would demand our return to work. We would have the green top and green shorts and white socks on and no one would blink an eyelid.

And when we got back to the ground we went back to abiding by Jock Stein's rulebook. It was his way or on your way.

We used to get all the dirty jobs to do. We would clean the boots of the players we liked. Tommy would always insist on cleaning the boots of the remaining Lisbon Lions. No boy born round the corner from St Mary's Church Hall, where Celtic were founded and where he would later be laid to rest, could resist that.

We would sit in the boot room on a Monday morning scrubbing, cleaning and talking football, hopes, dreams and aspirations.

But Tommy was mischievous and when we swept the terraces of bottles in the Rangers end after a game we brushed them into the stairwells. I would then fill a wicker basket and put it on my back to dump in a skip.

More often than not there would be the proverbial Buckfast bottle full of human piss lying around.

And Tommy would put that on top of the basket so it toppled onto my back halfway down the stairs. You'd feel that cold, wet but familiar sensation and you'd know Burns had done you again.

When I asked the boss if I could change my gear I would hide the reason I was so wet. If you misbehaved there was always the danger he'd get rid of you.

'Get fucking oot there and clean the terraces and shut up,' would be the answer. He could be unforgiving, big Jock.

Tommy was small and skinny and they were worried he would never develop. To Jock Stein he was always 'wee Tommy'.

For our first full pre-season Tommy and me were deemed too weak to do the full programme of running and hard work. I was six foot two but weak as a kitten and Tommy was like a waif and stray.

So Jock sent us to Butlins for the week. My mum and dad came down to see us for the day with Rena my future wife and Jim Brogan, a reserve player with a good head for business, gave us a few quids spending money. All Tommy did the whole time was talk about Celtic. Even as we laughed on the roundabouts, played the jukeboxes and eyed up the talent. We did what normal boys with Elton John platform shoes and bum fluff sideburns did. But we never crossed the line. It was more than our lives were worth.

The ground staff boys were never allowed to swear. Utter an oath and the big man would kick you out the door we were told; we never tested the matter.

If you approached the first team dressing room you knocked the door and waited until you were invited in. You lifted what you needed and you got out of there; this was not our environment, staying in there was a privilege that had to be earned.

You could not even listen to the conversations of the big names. Every now and then Jock would enter when we were in there, hear some bawdy talk or other and say, 'hey that's enough of that. Wait till the boys are out.' And you would be invited to leave so the chat could start again.

Jock was always stretching you, pushing you, looking for more. And God knows, you wanted to give him more; if you wanted to wear a green and white jersey you had precious little option.

If you really knew what was good for you, you also learned to lose at table tennis. Big Jock loved the game and after lunch he would stick his head round the door to order me or Tommy to play him.

The big face would glower at you if you beat him. He was a tippy tappy fancy sort of player who tried to hide the ball. He would have the jacket off with his big braces showing over his shirt and Sean Fallon his assistant would come in to watch. Every day of his managerial life big Jock was hindered by a limp sustained in the ankle injury, which ended his playing career at the age of 34. Because of that we would try to play sneaky low shots we knew he could not get down to. In an environment where winning was everything this was serious stuff and the games became a real event.

If he won a game it was all, 'NEXT! Come on Tommy, your turn to take a hammering son.' It was all roaring and laughing, great fun.

When we arrived at the club Willie Fernie the reserve coach took us under his wing. We were Willie's 'wee diamonds' as he called us and he would tell the big man, 'you won't beat my boys today.' If you beat him at lunchtime you would be hauled in at the end of the day before getting your bus so Jock could enact his retribution. When he was good big Jock was great. If you made him laugh you felt 100 feet tall.

Equally, when Jock was enraged it was not unlike rousing the devil in miniature. I got the end of it more than once because of my laid-back attitude. But even Tommy incurred the wrath from time to time.

When we were still just kids we turned up to see the squad list for an evening reserve game had been pinned up on the notice board. We were still at the bottom of the food chain, but there would always be a couple of kids taken along for the ride. And this night, to our glee, right there at the end of 17 names were 'A. Ritchie and T. Burns'.

We went home as happy as sandboys before returning to the ground that night to prepare for the game at 6.15pm.

It was a brisk winter's evening and Tommy turned up in the Parkhead foyer without a big coat. Catching glance of this, Big Jock turned and berated him.

'What do you think you are playing at turning up without a coat?' he roared. 'Do you think you're playing tonight or something? You turn up with no coat on a cold night like this to sit up in the stand? Is this you turning on the big-time routine Burns, do you think you've made it? Nae coat? Who do you think you are?'

And all I could do was stand there thanking the lord almighty that I had my coat; that it was not me being made to feel two feet tall.

Naturally Tommy and I were left out the team; there would be no need to remove my winter garments – that much had already been made clear.

We had the job of collecting the strips and making sure every player had what he needed and so on. We were back to being ground staff boys again.

We froze through the game with Tommy thoroughly depressed about the whole experience and dreading the next day at the park. Sure enough, next morning I was sitting alone in the boot room cleaning the debris of the previous night's game when the door opened and the manager's giant head appeared.

'Where is he?' he asked.

'He's doing something else,' I piped up, summoning every ounce of my being to open my parched mouth.

'You take note of that,' he added. 'You bring a coat to the games and never assume anything. I'll be speaking to him again when I see him about it.'

'Boss,' I said as boldly as I could muster, 'Thomas has not got a coat. His faither's not in the house any longer and there are no brothers. His mother cannae afford a coat.'

I said it as much for something to say; for the experience of talking to the man I still thought of at that point as Mr Stein.

There was a momentary silence then a grunt before the door shut.

A week later Tommy received his wages as usual and inside the brown packet was extra money for a coat – significantly more money.

He immediately took a bus up to Dees of the Trongate in the town centre and bought himself a long, wine coloured, John Shaft coat like in the films. It was the garb every young boy coveted and it did not come cheap.

Some folk would have spent £20 on a plain black garment and handed the rest to their mother. But Tommy had been told to buy a coat with the money and what Tommy was told Tommy did.

So he spent every penny of it on the most ostentatious number money could buy. When I think of it to this day it brings me close to tears because I can see Thomas now, proud as punch in that wine leather coat. We were more used to buying our casuals from the 'Crazy House' in Glasgow Cross – a shop more suited to what you might call the budget conscious purchaser.

I suspect big Jock always privately intended most of that money for Mrs Burns, Tommy's mother. But we were young, we were daft. We did not do subtlety. He went from having no coat one week to having the most expensive jacket at Celtic Park in a seven-day period. Kenny Dalglish and guys like that must have been looking and wondering how a skinny kid from the east end could afford a coat like that.

But we never got above ourselves. Willie Fernie was a lovely man and a great Celtic servant during two spells at the club as a player and he made sure of that.

Willie would tell us that we had already done the easiest part of the job. Getting to Celtic was one thing; staying there was a different matter.

I remember myself and Tommy listening to that kind of talk with cloth in our ears, we had always told ourselves that getting inside Celtic Park was the hardest part. As it worked out, Willie was right. Of course he was; what Willie Fernie did not know about life at Parkhead was not worth knowing.

Eventually we would see it his way. We'd sit in the boot room with our hopes and dreams imagining what it would be like to get a full-time contract. This, now, was the Holy Grail.

Rab Prentice and Brian McLaughlin were that bit older and one day they got their full-time contracts. Suddenly they were getting changed at 9.45am to go training with the big boys – no more cleaning boots for them.

That left three of us from my ground staff intake awaiting our fates; myself, Tommy and Jimmy Kyles. The other two were big-time now.

We badly wanted to join them and eventually the day arrived when big Jock would sit along the dusty corridor decreeing our respective fates.

The manager's door opened and we heard Jock's voice resonating like sandpaper in our direction.

'THOMAS, THOMAS BURNS.'

Away went Tommy in a state of near paralysis telling us he was sure this was it; he had been freed. We cajoled him out the door in his panicked state telling him he would get another year and would be back with us in no time. Like you do.

Ten minutes passed before he bounded back along the corridor beaming, cheeks burning as red as his flaming hair. 'I am going to Celtic Boys' Club,' he said, delighted with what constituted a step up for the youngest of our number.

Tommy was back on the ground staff for another year and we were staying together. Or so we hoped.

'ANDY, ANDY RITCHIE,' came the booming voice from the manager's office.

It was my turn for judgment and suddenly I am filled with doubt, thinking, 'Jesus, they can't keep all three of us on.'

They always freed one kid every year. That's how it worked.

In I went to see big Jock with Sean Fallon his assistant telling me they wanted more from me and that things were about to change for me. I feared the worst.

Wrongly as it happened. They were actually sending me out to Rob Roy Juniors in Kirkintilloch for more experience. I was coming out the Boys' club and was being farmed out to the juniors – a common step up for future first team prospects in those days.

'Was that alright?' I was asked. Damned right it was alright. The likes of Kenny Dalglish had been sent to Cumbernauld United and ended up in the first team – I had another year!

I ran back to the boot room and Tommy and I were hugging and dancing like we had won the Pools.

Then came the final call.

'JIMMY, JIMMY KYLES.' And we remembered our other pal in the room.

Tommy and I were on cloud nine, we had no fears for anybody, we were all flying through this. Jimmy, we felt, was destined for elevation to the reserves before us and the next 10 minutes flew past with me and Tommy planning our next moves, chatting excitedly about the future at Celtic.

Quarter of an hour passed, and still there was no Jimmy. So we sneaked out of the boot room and heard noises from the upholstered seat, which used to face the old main door at Celtic Park.

And there was Jimmy Kyles, head in hands, crying uncontrollably.

He had been freed and was heading back to the junior ranks in Dundee. The game was up, the dream was over.

These days you see men and women on the BBC News wailing in the aftermath of a death in Iraq or Afghanistan – and on reflection now this was a similar scene.

Nothing could have prepared me for what happened next. Within 10 seconds of approaching Jimmy there was Tommy Burns on the arm of the leather chair, crying and wailing and hugging our pal. The two of them were inconsolable.

To this day I remember feeling an acute sense of discomfort with this. I stood there frozen to the spot shuffling from foot to foot.

Ten minutes before, Tommy had been elated beyond all reason. And now here he was in a state of abject distress as if he had been the recipient of bad news rather than Jimmy.

Looking back all these years later I can now see that Tommy could empathise all too well with what Jimmy was feeling. Celtic was Tommy's life and it might just as easily have been him heading for the exit door. The margin for error was so slight.

Tommy had wanted it so much and here now was all the emotion, all the relief and all the empathy of the man coming out. He had thought this was to be his fate and perhaps driven by some form of catholic guilt Tommy kept in contact with Jimmy for years after that day.

I remember thinking that here, beyond all reasonable doubt, was the evidence of just what being at Celtic meant to Tommy.

Had that been me in Jimmy's shoes I would have felt gross disappointment for me and my mother and father. But that would have been it. Crying? Wailing? That's not for me thanks.

But Tommy? He would have been devastated and would have stayed on to help Hughie Snodgrass, the old linesman, cut the grass if it meant serving Celtic Football Club in some capacity. He lived the place; he breathed it with an intensity bordering on the messianic.

As events worked out oiling up a lawnmower was never necessary. Tommy and I played a couple of games in the reserve team together and he moved up to spend a spell at Maryhill Juniors in the north of Glasgow.

Everything was going fine for us both. I began getting more regular games for the reserves where I tried my damndest to impress.

Tommy, the ultimate Celtic man, gave me a bit of advice one day.

'Please the Jungle,' he said, 'and you'll be fine. If the Jungle love you, you're made for life.'

For the uninitiated I should explain that 'The Jungle' was one of the most formidable football terraces ever built. It was little more than a corrugated shed running along the Janefield Street side of Celtic Park, with a cemetery behind it. More than one playing career died a death at the hands of the Jungle Jims who packed themselves tightly into this lengthy stretch.

This old paddock held around 8,000 fans on a good day, but Jesus, these guys were the hardcore. The place could reverberate and rock to a beat more intimidating than anything the old Glasgow Apollo ever drummed up.

Tommy was right, if they did not like you the game was up. Even a Motherwell fan like me knew that.

So when I was named in the next reserve game after my pal's little pearl of wisdom I ran out determined to put on a show in my position as inside-right.

In those days all the games were played at Celtic Park and such was the quality of the reserve team and the lack of football on television that you could easily get 5,000 fans there. There may even have been more than that waiting to be impressed among my new target audience.

When the game started I tried a flick and a feint, all the tricks I knew to get the Jungle onside. To no avail. It was not going well.

It did not matter what I did, at every turn all I heard echoing through the chill air were derogatory shouts.

'GET RITCHIE AFF.'

'YOU'RE HOPELESS RITCHIE, YOU COULDNAE TRAP A COLD.'

'YOU'LL NEVER BE A PLAYER RITCHIE.'

I was desperate to please my newfound detractors. But whatever I did served only to make the abuse worse and I suffered a nightmare. It was later, as I tried to recover from my ordeal, that I learned where the barracking had been emanating from.

Tommy Burns and Gerry Collins, close friend, Soho Street neighbour and future fellow pro had paid their way in specially to give me pelters. That pair of bastards had done me over like a kipper.

I can laugh now. Insecure and uncertain of my future, I certainly did not at the time.

Chapter Four

Into the Elephant's Graveyard

IF TRUTH be told the real problems for me began when I made the Celtic first team.

I was fast-tracked beyond my years or level of maturity. Not that I thought so at the time. Self-belief was never a problem for me; I believed I could mix it with the big boys.

Billy McNeill was the captain and I knew Billy's parents from Bellshill. It would be a fabrication if I said I knew Billy when I went to Celtic as a kid. But I felt he looked out for me.

I got a game one day for the reserves when they still played bounce games between the first and second teams. I was not even in the reserves as such, I was only 16.

But big Jock Stein told me to get my kit on and go up against Billy. Imagine this; me the gangling kid against the man who had lifted the European Cup in Lisbon and was the ultimate Celt.

Big Jock had clearly told big Billy to give me a kick up the posterior. And everywhere else on my anatomy as well; he crawled all over me, he butted me, he shoved me and stuck his big jutting knee in my back. He gave me an hour of sheer hell.

But this was me learning what football among the big boys was all about. It was not about scoring eight goals for Celtic Boys Club and beating some team 10–0. This was what you aspired to; to give as good as you got to the Billy McNeills of this world.

This was learning on the job; youth development the way it used to work. These days they sit in an office staring at a computer and decide the next stage of a 16-year-old's development. Back then you learned in the school of hard knocks.

I must have learned reasonably well. I had a prolific spell alongside my Celtic teammate Joe McKee at Rob Roy at the beginning of the 1972–73 season when I scored 33 goals in 21 games with the minimum of fuss.

Celtic could not ignore me any longer. I was recalled from Kirkintilloch in February 1973 and, from there, progress was rapid. I started scoring goals in the reserves and by the end of the year I was ready.

I had been included in the party to travel to Finland for a European Cup game against FC Turun in September. I took this as a sign of my rising status.

Finally, I was named on the bench for the last game of 1973 against Dunfermline.

In my mother's old cuttings there is a picture of me jumping for joy at the news – heavily staged in that hackneyed way sports photographers always seem to favour. The only thing missing was a bag of balls.

The journalist who wrote the accompanying piece, the late James 'Solly' Sanderson of the *Daily Express*, would become a distinctive and legendary voice on Radio Clyde's *SuperScoreboard* phone-in. Back then, however, he hailed me as the face of the New Year.

'The spirit of football for 1974 is typified by 17-year-old Andy Ritchie of Celtic,' he wrote.

'For last night manager Jock Stein named the boy from Bellshill as substitute for today's final game of 1973 against Dunfermline at Parkhead.

'Stein, looking ahead to a bright new football year, told me; 'If things go right for us I will most certainly put Ritchie on.

'We all agree our game needs new faces, personalities and youth.

'I think it is fitting that a young man, who can typify football as we want to see it in 1974, should get his place.

'If we are playing well I will certainly bring on Andy. Scotland need the bright boys of tomorrow on the field today.'

This General Kitchener type address was heady stuff for a teenage debutant. Typical of the kind of thing Jock did when he wanted to drum up some positive publicity for the club.

To my relief the game did go well and I did get on. What the manager had not told me was that I would take my bow as a substitute for the legendary skipper Billy McNeill – the man who had given me that early grounding on first team training ground etiquette.

It was quite a moment when Jock Stein took off the captain of the Lisbon Lions to put me on instead.

People thought, 'geez, this must be some player this kid.' The minute the substitute's board went up I could virtually hear a collective intake of breath. Myself and Paul Wilson were the two subs that night and by the time I got on the game was well won.

But I can still hear Jock Stein saying to me; 'Go on, on you go.' He turned to Neillie Mochan the first team trainer and told him to get me sorted out. The rest passed in a bit of a blur, other than the moment when big Billy's number five board went up to gasps from the terraces. One of the greatest Celts ever was being replaced by a 17-year-old rookie.

David Hay – another future Celtic manager and colleague of mine – was moved to centre-half and I went to inside-right.

I remember hitting one from 25 yards which the Dunfermline 'keeper Geir Karlsson somehow tipped over the bar. I had another couple of rasping shots afterwards, which had the crowd raising eyebrows.

The big man simply said; 'well done.' Nothing more, nothing less. But that was enough for me.

When a manager is as decorated and as demanding as Jock Stein every word of praise is like a concerto to the ears. I can only imagine how the incomparable Lisbon Lions felt when that man praised their, 'pure, beautiful, inventive' football after they won the European Cup, the ultimate achievement at club level in world football.

I will lay you a dollar to a doughnut that they would have felt as if they could fight King Kong after every morsel of praise.

You craved it; if you got the slightest bit of credit from a man of that calibre it was incomparable; it was the highest high. I can hardly describe how good I felt when it happened after that debut appearance.

You had to earn your praise because everyone knew we were the best around. High standards were taken for granted, the minimum demanded.

People sometimes asked me, 'why did you go to Celtic?' The answer was simple; they had the best players. You wanted to go there as a kid to be around Jock Stein and the great players. In football that never changes.

Ask a kid in England if he wants to sign for Manchester United now or take first team football at Northampton. He'll take his chances at Old Trafford. Why? Well, the money is better for a start. But he also wants to be the one to please Sir Alex Ferguson or slip into the wind stream of Wayne Rooney.

The best young players go to the European Cup winners and when I went to Celtic in 1971 the club had been in two of the last five finals, winning one of them.

There was also the chance to play in Old Firm games against Rangers; the greatest derby in the world.

I eventually made my Old Firm debut in 1976 in one of my meagre 10 first-team appearances. We lost 2–1 and I had a chance to beat the Rangers 'keeper Peter McCloy before the ball stuck between his legs. I had missed a chance for immortality in the eyes of the Celtic support. On such moments do Celtic careers stand or fall.

But my problems had started before then; the moment Jock signed a guy by the name of Atholl Henderson from St Johnstone for a fee of £35,000.

He started to play this guy in the reserve team before me. And that was when I developed an attitude; a distinctly bad attitude. The facts to me remain thus; Atholl Henderson was a lovely fella – but he was not a 10th of the player I was.

I wish I could lay the blame for the way I reacted to his arrival at the doors of others; that I was influenced externally or easily led. But I was not – I acquired it all by myself.

It was maybe a safety net for me to behave like that. On reflection I clearly had insecurities and feared that deep down I was not good enough. So I developed this defensive mechanism to deal with it.

In retrospect I still wonder if Stein was setting me another target when he signed Henderson. One I was finally destined to fall short of.

Whenever Tommy Burns was set a target he got there. He maybe struggled and had to work at it, but he got there. In contrast I had reached all my targets until then with the minimum of fuss.

It felt easy for me. People might see me as holding a major candle for myself when they read that, but it was a simple and transparent fact at the time. Not many kids make their debut for Celtic at 17.

It all came easy to me whereas it was different for Tommy. He was almost propelled out the door so many times when they thought he would not develop physically.

But it was easy for me and as my father, an inherently wise man, was fond of saying; 'easy come, easy go'.

I did not really have to put the work in. So maybe Atholl Henderson was there to extract more effort from me. Maybe he was my next target; to drive me closer to 25 goals a season for the Celtic first team.

Atholl played no more than two games for the first team by my recollection. But one thing became clear; he had quickly gone beyond me in the pecking order and I did not like it.

'How could they do that to me?' became my mantra. What I should have been saying was, 'excuse me Atholl, you're on my turf,' whilst elbowing him aside with my ability.

Looking back now an experienced Tommy Burns, in his days as Celtic manager, might have been able to articulate all this to me.

But he could not save me from myself back then; he was only a kid like me. There was nobody there telling us what big Jock was up to.

That was the way football was in those days. There were no sports psychologists to gee you up, no agents to take your views to the manager and demand that your ego be massaged.

If you were lucky you learned all that from the experienced pros. I learned some stuff from Jim Brogan and Tommy Callaghan in the reserves. But there was no one to tell me when Jock Stein was putting me to the test; trying to wind me up, find out what I was really made of. Not even at home.

My dad was a lovely man and I would never criticise him. He was a Motherwell supporter who worked six days a week at Rolls-Royce. He was a good man, a fine father. But deep down he knew little about football beyond what I told him.

And what a teenage footballer with an ego tells you is not always the best information.

So even at home I had little advice imparted to me. There was no one bombarding me with well meaning pearls of wisdom. God, how I needed them. I was losing my way fast.

My brother Liam, best man at my wedding to Rena, recently reminded me of the day things quite clearly began to change for me. In the summer of 1974 if I recall correctly. The day when football suddenly became an uphill struggle after years of smooth, streamlined progress.

Celtic played a pre-season friendly against Preston North End, where Bobby Charlton, now a 'Sir', was the player-manager. And I was pitched directly up against him in right-midfield.

I fancied my chances of showing this old fella how to play this game. Can you imagine? Me, this cocky young buffoon, believing I could teach a World Cup winner – one of the finest footballers in England's history – how to suck eggs.

In 70 minutes on the same pitch I barely got a kick at the ball. He showed me everything there is to know about playing football.

He dropped his shoulders and I could not get near him. I even resorted to trying to kick this venerable veteran of the English game; by then I was desperate. Bobby administered to me an education on the game at the age of 36. How to get into space, use it, shrug off your opponent, pass the ball and use it properly.

They had a boy playing on the other wing by the name of Tony Morley, later to make his name at Aston Villa. And Charlton would switch the play to him quick as a dart. He was a fantastic two-footed maestro, a real football player.

And I left the pitch that day; head down, thinking to myself, 'this game is going to be more difficult than I ever imagined'.

If I touched the ball four times then I certainly did not touch it five. In the pit of my stomach I knew something had changed, that the upward spiral had slowed. This was a different ball game altogether.

This man had won a World Cup and a European Cup medal at Wembley. And, here in his advancing years, I had said to myself; 'this won't be a problem to the likes of me'. How wrong can you be?

It annoyed me afterwards that I had allowed my pre-match arrogance to overcome my abilities. When Charlton left the field with 20 minutes to go I was relieved, delighted even. Respite at last.

I had been through the reserves and the youth set-up; I had climbed every mountain placed in my way. I had made an impression on the older boys in the reserve team – I was on their tail and they knew it. But this? This was a whole new ball game – one with which I was wholly unfamiliar.

Maybe I was being too hard on myself. Bobby Charlton had embarrassed better players than me. But, Jesus, that one hurt. So much so that my own brother still sees it as a turning point for me at Celtic.

Despite it all Jock Stein still wanted to give me a new four-year contract before I finally said enough was enough.

Morton had come in for me in October 1976 for a few thousand quid and a drop in wages. I had developed the bad attitude with bells on by then. I was a work in progress and the screws were coming loose.

How can I put this? I was a cheeky, arrogant prick. I can put it no other way.

I was married in November 1975 in Uddingston and I wanted to play football and earn some win bonuses. I was under no pressure from Rena, my childhood sweetheart – she told me not to go. But the morning after the reception I was ordered to join the reserves for a trip to Perth to play St Johnstone. Not the first team, the reserves. And I wanted more.

Falkirk had tried to sign me a couple of seasons before for £50,000. At that point my stock was rising. Jock Stein had told me about the bid and asked me what I thought. I had shrugged and indicated general indifference; I did not want to leave Celtic at the time.

'You're no' going to fucking Falkirk,' was the Big Man's final word on the matter. And that had been that.

But this time it was different. I wanted first-team football and the chance of the occasional win bonus.

Jock Stein had been in a serious car crash the year before, returning in the early hours of 5 July from a holiday with his wife and friends on a Spanish island. His Mercedes was carrying him, his bookmaker friend Tony Queen, Mrs Stein and two passengers in the back when another car drove at him up the wrong direction on a dual carriageway and struck close to Lockerbie on the notorious M74.

The Big Man was touch and go initially and was gravely ill for most of the 1975–76 season. The impact on Celtic was enormous. We struggled through a year or so of Sean Fallon deputising, with different ideas and ways of doing things.

During Jock's recovery period Sean took me along with the squad for a European game in East Germany to play a Cup-Winners' Cup quarter-final game against Sachenring Zwickau. It was a 3pm kick-off on a Wednesday because they had no floodlights and the game was being beamed back live on television – an unusual state of affairs in those days.

I did not feel at my best. I had a bad throat, which I felt was no impediment to playing. Nothing short of involuntary paralysis would have stopped me from playing a game in Europe. But Sean called the doctor and I was placed in quarantine. Under protest it should be said.

At one point in the game I remember the central defender Roddy MacDonald playing centre-forward. To my mind I could have played that day. I could have been that man; should have been indeed.

I might not have done myself justice with a bad throat, but I never felt the need to be quarantined, with a defender playing striker instead. It was an over-reaction and we lost 1–0 and limped out of Europe once more after a 1–1 draw in Glasgow.

There and then I became convinced that Sean was looking for reasons not to play me. Paranoid? Possibly, but this was me at that time; I had a chip on each shoulder.

Before Jock's car accident I felt as if I was being groomed for the first team. Maybe I was wrong, but I felt wanted and valued. And that feeling was slipping away and I did not like it.

I had my first-team highlights. The best memory was scoring the winner in Aberdeen as a sub in a League Cup game when we won 2–1 and Bobby Lennox scored the first goal.

I loved being involved. These days kids come through and play at 16 or 17 at Celtic and Rangers. In those days you just did not do that – not under the incomparable Jock Stein. You had to earn the right. Celtic jerseys, as the big man would say, did not shrink to fit inferior players.

My old ground staff colleague Brian McLaughlin had got there before me – but I was coming along behind him at the speed of a jump jet. Even the great players of the Quality Street era such as Danny McGrain, Lou Macari and David Hay were lucky to make their debuts before they were 21.

But here was I as a 17-year-old being spoken about in the same company as the greats of Celtic Park and that felt special. Even to sit with these men of a Lisbon vintage was an education and I felt incredibly privileged to have that granted to me. Here I was living the dream of so many young men in the West of Scotland. And yet after scaling the peak I was sliding back down as my 20th birthday approached.

In Jock's absence my chances to impress receded.

When he did come back it was hard for me to judge any difference in the man. I was too young to remember the firebrand genius of 1965, when he had lifted the Scottish Cup to trigger a landslide of trophies, or '67 in Lisbon. I knew him only from the day I walked in through the gates of paradise in 1971.

From that day he had been the most powerful influence in my life; he was the fulcrum of the entire club. He had taken time out to recuperate from the crash, but like all football people he did not take enough time. They never do.

Physically he seemed to me to be recovering slowly, but mentally he seemed the same man. He still had the same influence, but somehow he was not the same manager. Quite how or why I cannot entirely explain. Sean Fallon would say later that he was quiet, that he had lost his sparkle. But here was a man who had rattled out nine Championships in a row. He was untouchable. He had set the marker for every Celtic manager for decades to follow. Who was in a position to judge him?

Certainly not me. But it did become apparent to me that we were having problems with our relationship. There were too many rows and arguments, too much tension.

I felt all of a sudden that I was no longer the golden boy, I was no longer being marked out for greatness.

Davie McParland arrived at the club as Jock's new assistant with Sean shunted aside to head up the scouting operation. If anything that made matters worse.

Davie had a different way of looking at things. He made instant judgements and knew little of what had gone before; he neither knew nor cared for the story of young Andy Ritchie, the future of Celtic.

He brought in a new outlook and more than one Partick Thistle player. He had managed there and one or two of these guys fancied themselves after winning the League Cup in 1971. The Johnnie Gibsons and Joe Craigs and Ronnie Glavins appeared one by one and they were favourites of his.

I do not think Davie especially liked me if truth be told. Looking back now he might not have been wrong in that.

But at the time, I felt I was doing enough – the evidence suggested otherwise. I was working my way backwards and had slipped behind others in the orderly queue for first team places. Or indeed the reserve team.

I was developing the attitude, which did me few favours.

I remember the day Jock phoned me to tell me Morton had come in for me. It was a Wednesday and I was on a day off at home in the flat Rena and I had in Cumbernauld.

It was before 9am and I picked up the phone to a gruff, unforgiving greeting.

'You not out your fucking bed yet?' he growled. There was no breezy good morning, no small talk about the contents of the papers or the unseasonal weather.

I knew immediately who was on the line. Life at that time did not revolve around niceties in football.

'Get your big fat arse into Celtic Park,' added the boss. 'You said the other day you wanted to move on. I might be able to help you.'

And down went the phone with a bump. There was nothing resembling a farewell or an urging to drive safely. He was right, I had knocked on his door, I had spoken of my desire to move on. And now my bluff was being called.

I arrived at Parkhead to find Jock sorting out a deal for Morton goalkeeper Roy Baines in an effort to fill a long-term problem position following the retirement of Ronnie Simpson. I, apparently, was going the other way whether I liked it or not.

There was no respect for individual feelings or discussions with an agent. I saw the Morton chairman Hal Stewart sitting there and it was clear what was happening. If truth be told, I had no real objections to the idea.

John Clark, the legendary defender and newly appointed reserve coach, was called in. And I was told I did not have to go. I then went to the ubiquitous Joe's Kitchen, where all the big deals were done, to talk with Hal. He sold me a dream quite outwith the realities of life in Greenock. There would be a couple of thousand pounds in a signing on fee. And he would utilise his fellow Morton directors to get me a job driving a van to ease the transition from full to part-time football. When we got up to the Premier League, he told me, we'd move to full-time football.

Most of all, though, I would be involved in something big. I am damned if I knew what I was going to be involved in. But he was looking for a striker, I could score goals and here was a man with a first-class degree in bullshit.

Hal was like some lovable grandfather. He was full of charm, a perfect gentleman and an entrepreneur. He had fingers in many pies and he was never slow in telling you of his influence at the American Tobacco Company, organising football nights to sell cigarettes. He was a softhearted Bing Crosby type who loved his golf. He spent his life talking up Morton. He had brought the first Danes such as Kai Johannson and Eric Sorenson to Scotland and sold them on for a generous profit. At one point he trumpeted six Danes playing for Morton in a game against Hearts. He was a born, natural showman.

I do not think for a minute that Hal Stewart signed me that day thinking that I would one day earn him a top table seat at the Sports Writers' Award dinner for Player of the Year. Or lead Morton to the top of the Premier League.

He gave the same chat to everybody. Some you never heard of again in your life. A good salesman gives the same pitch time after time with the same degree of enthusiasm. So I don't think he saw anything great in me to any great degree. I was just another body he could get in for a few quid and sell on for a few more. It would not have mattered if I was Andy Ritchie the footballer or Hercules the Bear. If Hal saw a couple of quid in you, the world was your oyster. He would have been the ultimate Scottish agent, had there been such a thing at the time. Bill McMurdo or Willie McKay multiplied by 50 times. He talked the talk and gave me the impression he could also walk the walk.

And there was Rena drawing me daggers. Her views on the matter were clear.

'You don't have to go,' she implored, kicking me under the table. 'Stay at Celtic, we'll sort it out.'

I never was much of a listener. I went back to Celtic Park and told them of my desire to go. What happened then took me aback.

'I'll tell you what I'll do,' said Jock reaching for a stack of paper. 'There's a new four-year contract on the table here. If you sign it we'll start all over again fresh. All the stuff that's gone before will be in the past. You can get yourself back in and get fit and we'll say no more about it.'

There would be no pay rise in it for me. I would still be on £40 a week – though if I got in the first team there would be more for me. They would sort out the bonuses and I would receive a £1,000 signing on fee.

But we never got to that stage. I wanted to play every week, score goals, make a name for myself and resurrect my career.

I did not want to sign up again and find myself in exactly the same position 12 months later. It mattered little what my wife said, my mind was made up.

Incredulous I had turned down his contract offer Jock was by now scathing: 'Do you really want to go to that Elephant's Graveyard?' he had asked me.

But Haldane Y. Stewart, the Morton chairman who could sell sand to the Arabs, had convinced me I was the best player since Pele.

And in return for losing me big Jock was happy to take Roy Baines. Celtic, in fact, would finish up paying Morton £10,000 to do the deal.

I had played against the young Morton manager Benny Rooney once or twice and knew he was a go-ahead ambitious sort.

There were last minute doubts, but not many. I had made Hal Stewart a promise and I kept to it. I signed for Morton and made my debut at Cappielow the following Wednesday.

Chapter Five

When Cultures Collide

MY INITIAL impression of Cappielow was unfavourable.

To me it seemed as if the Vikings had just looted the main stand and headed for the escape boats 20 minutes prior to my arrival. And the sensual assault was not entirely visual either.

'Christ,' I thought, 'this place stinks of gas.'

They had an old fire in the corner of the dressing room and it was leaking. Little wonder, with Morton second bottom of the Second Division on my arrival, that some players almost seemed to be sleepwalking onto the park.

My thought process was probably on a par with General Custer at Little Bighorn.

'What the f*** have I done here?' was the gist of it. Celtic Park was no Bernabeu at that time. But the South Stand had been fairly recently rebuilt, while here I found myself in an old ground reeking of decay, crying out for some tender loving care.

I remember meeting my great boyhood hero, the former Motherwell striker John Goldthorpe, as I walked in.

'Andy, what you doing down here?' he asked me.

'I'm playing against Clydebank tonight John,' I replied.

'You're whit?' he asked, face creasing with incredulity. 'What? Are you down on loan?'

'Naw,' I responded, alarmed by his response, 'I signed for Morton this afternoon.'

At which point my idol floored me with his parting shot.

'What the f*** did you sign down here for?' he asked, before turning away towards the dressing room. As recommendations go, this was a discouraging start.

'Goldie' became my travelling companion from Lanarkshire for 19 months. And for the first six to eight months of that period my fitness was impeccable. Cappielow was no place for the light-hearted, but it was home and I was here to play football to the best of my ability. How else could I hope to get out of there as quickly as possible?

The first game I played that night against Clydebank saw me go up against a player by the name of Davie Cooper. Coops was a fantastic entertainer, a winger of the old school and his death towards the end of a dazzling career a real blow to Scottish football.

But that night I did not know either him or my own teammates from Adam. I was feeling my way, with around 1,400 at the game – a similar crowd to a Celtic reserve game on a winter's night in November.

The weather in Greenock was true to form. The wind blew, the rain came down horizontally in sheets, the light was gloomy and the crowd deeply subdued. I gave them little to wake them from their slumber as I recall, but personally I was pleased to be playing.

The real culture shock arrived on the Saturday when we went to Love Street to play St Mirren, our greatest rivals. The old Renfrewshire derby can be a ferocious affair and the glowering mood of my new fan base was not lightened that day by a thumping 5–1 defeat to a team managed by a certain Alex Ferguson esq.

They were a good team with players on the make such as Lex Richardson and Tony Fitzpatrick and they would run away with the League that season. To say I did not enjoy that game would be putting it lightly. Once again, after placing my initial misgivings to the back of my mind, an old question was rising to the fore.

'What have I done here?' was all I could ask myself as I drove home, the sense of weighty depression, which would become familiar to me in later years, blackening my journey. On leaving Celtic I had told myself I had to take one step backwards to take two forward. That night I felt as if I had taken four backwards with no prospect of gaining so much as a solitary stride.

But the games came thick and fast. We trained on the Tuesday night and were back in on Wednesday to play Montrose at home.

I scored twice and hit the first of my trademark free-kicks for the club. The weather was similar to the previous Wednesday; it was a dark, gloom-laden winter night. But somehow I was finding comfort in my football. And in a new mental mantra which, if truth be told, had been inspired by that terrible mauling in Paisley.

'I better get my finger out here,' I had said to myself on the Saturday night and every day since. 'I don't want to be hanging about here too f*****g long.'

But the team I played with at St Mirren was not the same team I would go on to do great things with at Morton. There was deadwood in that dressing room that had to be cleared away and well Benny Rooney, my new manager, knew it.

Morton was Benny's first managerial posting and there was a brightness, a freshness about him. His father Bob Rooney had been the physio at Celtic and I had seen him in and around Parkhead even after he had left as a player. He came to a lot of the Celtic reserve games. I had also played against him at St Johnstone at the old Muirton when he had been in the reserves for a few games.

My ex-wife Rena also worked in the optician's upstairs from Benny's wife's hairdressing salon. So, as he dropped his wife off to open up I would drop off my good lady and we got to know each other.

Benny had spoken to me about coming to Morton long before Hal Stewart rolled up at Celtic Park, if truth be told. Would I come down to Greenock with him? he'd ask. And because Benny was a smashing guy I thought it was a great idea. But to all intents and purposes it was pie in the sky until Jock Stein decided Roy Baines could do him a job in goal.

As Hal blustered that day I signed, Benny was in the back of my mind. The man had a football career behind him, he was a good friend of Billy McNeill, and he was bringing a freshness to the whole environment at Morton.

He had been granted a blank sheet of paper and been allowed to reshape the club. And I sometimes look back at Benny's managerial career and feel it mirrors my own experience at the club; he began with so much promise, he was a smart young man, he looked at situations, sized them up and did a fantastic job in his early years in charge.

You always had the feeling that he had intelligence; that he knew what the game was all about. True, he signed up to that horrible trend of wearing bad camel-skin coats, which afflicted many managers of his time.

But he was good to work for, the kind of guy you would go into the trenches with. And I believe Morton suited Benny Rooney as much as he suited them.

Deep down, though, he made the same mistake as me; he should never have hung around there as long as he did. That was where it all went wrong. When he finally left Cappielow after giving his all he never really enjoyed a great deal of success. Again, a bit like myself.

At that time people did not give enough credit to the man for his achievements. Yes, Hal Stewart could sell ice to the Eskimos.

But it was Benny who moulded the football team. He chose the players Hal charmed. It was Benny who gave guys an opportunity to play and further their careers.

And so I realised something was taking shape at Morton reasonably quickly. That playing at the place might not be so bad after all.

We travelled up to Montrose on a Friday night for a First Division game in the 1976–77 season around the Christmas period to stay in a hotel. Prior to my arrival this, I was told, had been completely and utterly unheard of.

Staying in a local gaff ahead of a distant away game the night before had been standard practice at Celtic; anything else would have brokered a revolt.

Benny was trying to engender a sense of professionalism in the team. Little did he realise that all he was actually doing was subsidising a wild night out.

Two teammates of mine, the full-back Ian Sneddon and midfielder Jim Townsend, sneaked out the hotel at midnight to go for booze. The experienced guys who had floated around the lower reaches of the Scottish game were unused to this kind of privilege. And they were damned well intent on abusing it to the full.

For once I was in my bed by 10pm. I suppose I was not as wild then as I thought I was. But some of them were out until 5am drinking, carousing, getting up to god knows what. It was the kind of behaviour I would indulge in myself in time.

But at that time I was only six weeks out of Celtic. I had come from full-time training and I was the fittest I would ever be in my life.

I went down for breakfast and it quickly became apparent all was not entirely as it should be.

One of the aforementioned senior pros of the team was leaning over on a chair talking to a teammate. I was told Sneddon and Townsend had been out on the lash most of the night, arriving back at the hotel for a brief snatch of sleep before trekking downstairs resembling the cast of the Living Dead.

The advice I heard being imparted went as follows: 'Tell the gaffer you're not feeling very well. It'll be fine. He'll leave you out.'

What they had forgotten was that the chairs they were sitting on were high-backed. And they had not had the brains to peer around the high backs to see who might be sitting behind them.

Had they done so they would have witnessed Benny Rooney the manager, staring at them and listening to every word of the conversation. For him this was akin to a custard pie to the face, a splash of freezing cold water in a hot room. Suddenly he saw what had to be done to take the team forward.

These guys were finished. They were left out the team to play Montrose, a couple of young, hungry replacements coming in instead. As I had against Montrose in my second game at Cappielow I scored twice and we travelled back down through Dundee that night with the points in the bag. We were on a roll.

In contrast the miscreants concerned were living on borrowed time. Benny was sweeping through the first team like the proverbial hurricane. He was intent upon bringing younger, better players in.

He already had a spine to his team in the form of Jim Holmes and my boyhood hero Goldthorpe. He also brought in big Bobby Thomson from St Johnstone, a left-midfielder who proved a fantastic signing for Morton at £25,000.

A young Mark McGhee had been signed on a free transfer from Bristol City and had come back up the road. We played together in that first season along with other guys who were good, seasoned players at that level.

We had a scout in Greenock called Ronnie Alfield who watched young players in the area. If the best young players in the shadows of the shipyards could not play for Rangers or Celtic then they played for Morton. These days they disappear off to distant places like Ross County to avoid playing for Morton. But, as I say, these were less mercenary times.

Local boys like Neil Orr, George Anderson and Joe McLaughlin would come through in time and we were improving all the time.

The late Tommy Veitch came from Halifax, Jim Rooney came from Queen's Park and Benny made the most of a very limited budget.

He was adding bits and bobs and guys who could do a turn, even for a short time. Ally Scott came from Rangers and for me it was unusual to have another player with Old Firm experience roll up.

He arrived with a pedigree and, if truth be told, was far too sensible to be a football player. He was an educated man and was coming to Cappielow because he loved the game, not because he needed it.

So we were mixing a lot of characters to find the right blend.

We were never a bunch of guys destined to be bosom buddies exactly, but we rubbed along and we won football games.

From my perspective I finally had what I wanted; I was playing football every week, I was scoring goals.

Finally I was feeling as if I was back where I always planned to be; taking one step back to take two forward. To paraphrase George Peppard in the A-Team, the plan was coming together and I was loving it.

Financially, things were not great. The driving job Hal had promised me that fateful day in Joe's Kitchen, Parkhead, had failed to turn up.

Years later I would discover that Hal offered every new signing a day job in order to persuade them to go part-time at Cappielow.

It was a promise he was rarely able to keep. Unemployment was rife in Greenock and Port Glasgow at that time, the shipyard cranes were rusting with inactivity and the great yards such as Scott Lithgow were dying a lingering death.

Hal, as was his wont, had overstated his sway when he was offering people work. If the truth be told I was ill-equipped in terms of skills I could take into the job market in any case. But that would not stop Hal telling you otherwise to get you signed.

I managed to get work by myself in Glasgow's Gallowgate lifting animal carcasses from pillar to post. I also did spells of tarring the roads. How that would go down with insurers of highly paid players these days I would not like to say. I also sold lemonade and other soft drinks for Dunne & Moore. Anything to supplement my meagre Morton income.

It was an awkward situation. There was a sense of bewilderment at Hal's failure to come up with the job he had promised. It was the cause of one of the first – if not the last – argument I had with my now ex-wife.

By late 1976 I was scouting around desperately for cash to build up the marital nest. Rena had been there the day Hal had vowed to give me the earth, the moon and the stars. She always remembered broken promises with far greater precision than I ever did.

When they failed to materialise I, like so many players of my era, chose to conveniently forget them because the football was going alright. If I was earning a bonus winning a game and scoring a goal that was fine by me.

All the while Hal would be propping up the bar at the Stirling Castle Pub, near the Kelvin Hall, where the great and the good of Scottish football liked to hang out. Anyone who was anyone, be they chairmen, journalists or players hung out there. And while I would be looking for work Hal would no doubt be reeling in another new signing, offering them a driving job through a friend of a Morton director. It was the same spiel with the same results all the time.

Rena's work in the optician's was effectively bringing in the same kind of money as me. It was a poor state of affairs.

And yet so long as I was scoring goals, there was always the promise of something greater around the corner. I always felt one day that I was destined for bigger and better things than Morton. Our day would come.

It was not until years later that I learned of the fact that, after a couple of months at Morton, our day had come. And passed again with me none the wiser.

After my bright start to life in the First Division Jock Stein had attempted to take me back to Parkhead. Had I known of this at the time I would have created merry hell to secure my return to full-time football.

It was only many years after I had finished as a football player that I even learned of the bid from Sean Fallon. Jock was willing to pay £170,000 to return me to Paradise. The proviso was simple; Morton would be duty bound to clarify that I had only ever been 'on loan'.

It was a deception, but a lesser one than that perpetrated by Hal when he declined to inform me of the proposal either at the time or afterwards. I heard the news incredulously over a couple of beers and it was like taking a punch to the stomach followed by a swift uppercut as I rose to my feet. And I had never been terribly good at rolling with the blows.

I cannot say for certain if I am talking with the benefit of hindsight here, but soon after leaving Celtic I had begun to harbour a knotting in the stomach at the thought of a return to Parkhead. I can only describe it as a yearning. Finding out that I had been unwittingly denied my wish felt not unlike hearing of a compliment someone had given you 20 years ago previous. Someone you thought had never liked you in the first place.

Nice, flattering, heart-warming, but ultimately pointless. The moment had passed; the sentiments no longer meant a thing. It is difficult to explain in words. I just wish to Christ I had known at the time.

I quickly realised at Morton that I had never really wanted to leave Celtic. But things had gone so far; relations had soured so badly, that I really had to. I was putting pressure on myself to succeed and I had to get away; to reinvent myself.

Had Celtic paid close to £200,000 for me – a king's ransom in 1976 – then I have no doubts that my early status as a player to be groomed and nurtured would have returned. I would have been there as an established first team player on better money and with significantly more kudos behind me. Kenny Dalglish had already informed big Jock of his desire for a fresh start in England by then and would leave for Liverpool at the end of that season. There was, in short, a gap in the market for me to exploit. Had I been told, of course.

But Hal Stewart, an optimist to his bootstraps, was already harbouring notions of making me Scottish football's first £1 million player. Even if he was not exactly paying me the wages of a superstar.

Around that period our first son Mark was born and money became tighter still, but we kind of muddled along. Jobs were hard to keep, because they were jobs of convenience. You took on short-term gigs to fit with the football.

We had been promised full-time football at Morton, but – surprise, surprise – that never came to anything either. Precious few of the promises ever did.

Ian Archer, the late and much missed journalist and Morton supporter, thought the world of Hal. He saw everything that was good in football in the man and, conversely, everything that was going bad. And people loved him for his imperfections.

Even when we would turn up at Queen Street Station for a train to an away game at Aberdeen with 18 of us in the squad plus officials.

There might be 28 of us in all and Hal would brush his way past the ticket collector on the gate with a batch of tickets in the air yelling out, 'MORTON FOOTBALL CLUB' without allowing the poor fellow time to check them. If he had he would have discovered there were only five or six paid for billets in Hal's hand. But his slight of hand made it look good. Appearances were everything.

There's no such thing as a free lunch, they say, but Hal proved that theory wrong time and again. And yet he was never less than generous in his administration of alcohol. He was a great gin and tonic man who enjoyed the bonhomie of the golf club. He was old school to his bootstraps.

But you need not have bothered asking him for the fiver you had lent him at the bar three weeks previous. Or money from the club you had been promised verbally.

'Signing on fee is it Andy? What do you want? £500? No problem.'

Six weeks later a three-piece leather suite would arrive at your door, courtesy of the chairman of Morton. But that did not equate to £500 cash. We already had a sofa – we needed the money thanks. But Hal was the managing director of the Co-operative Society at that time and it was more expedient for him to send round cheap furniture than it was a cheque.

Smoke and mirrors was always the way with Haldane Y. He could just as easily have been a magician.

So far as supporters were concerned there was a kind of magic working at Morton in any case. And Hal was the big top promoter in the hat drawing them in to see the show.

By the end of my first season we had put together a run of 16 games unbeaten to storm up the table and finish fourth.

Yet that cut little ice with the tipsters when it came to the start of the 1977–78 season. The First Division, always a tough League, would pit us against the full-time talents of Hearts and Dundee. Part-timers like us, they said, did not stand a cat in hell's chance. We thought otherwise.

I had scored arguably the best goal of my career, a 40-yard howitzer against Watford, in pre-season. I felt I could take on the world and win.

On the first day of the new season we beat Kilmarnock 4–1 at Rugby Park. And as the bus trundled back up the A77 towards Glasgow, where most of the players were based, we knew we had played really well. McGhee and I were gelling, the team were coming together and we were onto something here.

In the Devil's Elbow, the old pub on the corner of George Square where the bus picked us up and dropped us off before and after games, they were quickly starting to talk of us as promotion possibles. Someone had to believe in us.

I felt that night after demolishing Killie that we would not be far away come the end of the season. We had added one or two new signings and augmented our end to the previous season.

But Hearts and Dundee were always going to be the favourites. Those two, ourselves and Kilmarnock quickly emerged as the front-runners in the title race for promotion to the Premier League.

But we lost to Hearts 3–0 in the League Cup to put a dent in our confidence. And when we played them in the League at Cappielow days later few fancied our chances.

When we streaked 3–0 up in jig time few could believe it. Hearts pulled a couple back, but we ran out 5–2 winners and I think I set up four of the goals. There were a few people rubbing their eyes at that result when Grandstand put up the final scores. Not least in Kilmarnock, where the local team's hopes of staying in the race had just taken an almighty blow to the temple.

Hearts and Dundee were big clubs playing full-time football. And Hal had told us that if we could get ourselves into the Premier League then the club would go full-time. For Morton that was the big carrot, but for the players in that team it was not a major consideration. Were I to say this was propelling us towards promotion I would be lying; the boys in that dressing room had their eyes on bigger fish. On big money moves down south or to the bigger clubs in the Premier League.

It was always nice to hear there was a full-time option if necessary. But we had a young team and they had one eye on Cappielow and another on the exit. Myself included.

Not to the extent where we took our eye off the ball however.

We sealed our entry to the Scottish Premier League on the second last day of the season. I scored a late penalty in a 3–1 win over Airdrie to win the Championship.

A year and a half after leaving Celtic I had recovered from my step backwards. I scored 26 goals that season. The result? I was back where I felt I belonged.

Chapter Six

Best in the Country

I ALWAYS remember Johnny Goldthorpe driving me to training at Morton one evening in our promotion season of 77–78.

Johnny was 32, had been a good pro and knew a thing or two about prolonging careers. I had always looked up to him until the day he turned to me in the car and said, 'you'll not last until you're 27 in this game'.

I was angry, furious in fact. I was not having that, not even from Johnny fucking Goldthorpe.

I was 20 at that time and I was flying. I was scoring goals, winning rave write-ups and was the best player in the country. What did this old fella know about anything?

Well, one thing he did know was the smell of drink when it reached his nostrils. And I was in that car passenger seat steaming drunk. I had been drinking all afternoon, and some of the morning as well. Was that unusual? Not especially. Not at all in fact.

I would still be stinking of drink when I played games. People used to call me the Idle Idol. And it ticked me off if truth be told. But after 30 years in denial I might as well accept now what others have always regarded as gospel.

'We never saw him the whole game,' they'd say. No wonder they never saw me, I was suffering a blinding hangover most of the time.

I was very good at getting to somewhere when the ball had just left. Ask anyone who has played with a massive hangover and they will tell you how that is done. Public parks across Britain are full of exponents of the art on a Sunday morning. The difference was that I was playing in the Scottish Premier League. And somehow I was still scoring goals. Extravagant goals as well.

People said I tried anything and that everything I hit came off for me. It would be suffice to say that I was playing most of the time with a hangover. Do not ask me why, but I thought that was smart behaviour. The done thing.

'I'll do whatever the fuck I want' summed up my attitude best. And bugger anybody who got in my way. Especially when I started scoring like no one's business in the Premier League. Especially when my goals were helping the team to the top of the League before Christmas and challenging for Europe.

I had my act down to an art form. I was a big fish in a small pond. At Celtic I had been the opposite. But even there the attitude was growing, developing, gnawing its way into my consciousness. I was starting to believe my own bullshit. Perhaps the best thing I can say in my own defence was that it never affected the football. Neither did I ever allow my sense of humour to slip through it all.

Big Jock Stein had told me towards the end of my time at Parkhead – because I had begun to develop an opinion by that time – that the best thing I could do was to take the cotton wool out of my ears and shove it in my fucking mouth.

Every night I went drinking and partying had its positives. I did not do it to blot out any pain, let me assure you of that. If it had been a tale of woe I would have stopped doing it.

But I saw no need. I had been boozing, gambling and doing whatever and we had still reached the promised land of the top tier.

As our first campaign with the big boys began we knew we were capable of taking on Rangers and Celtic. We never doubted it.

What we needed, however, was a similar leap of faith from the club. We needed Hal Stewart to walk into that dressing room and say, 'boys, you have earned the right to take this club to the next level. We're going full-time.'

I am not saying that would have been some cure-all or panacea. Or that it would have kept us together as a team indefinitely. But it might have made us an even tighter unit. It might have got me a Scotland cap. And it would almost certainly have taken Morton into Europe for the first time in our history. The club, for whatever reason, opted against fulfilling the vague verbal promises made previously. Hal palmed us off with airy-fairy stories and excuses. When a man can look you in the eye and tell you he will get you a full-time job the day he signs you – then shrug it off when he fails – then that is never likely to be a problem.

Even aside from the full-time aspect, we had to fight for every penny. We were never handed pots of gold as a thank you for what we did for the club. Benny Rooney had to fight for every sheckle.

But there was a secrecy to it all. We never knew what the others were earning in bonuses and that was no doubt deliberate. There was no flat rate, they just told you individually they were doing the best they could for you and that was that. They made it up.

A measure of the kind of thing Hal would do to palm you off still makes me laugh to this day.

Every Christmas time a local Greenock butcher would lay on a dozen free turkeys for the players to enjoy with our families.

But times moved on and by the time we were topping the Premier League in 1979 we had a squad of 18 players. And our local benefactor was unwilling to budge. We had always received 12 turkeys and that was what we would continue to receive.

Thankfully for Hal a Levi denim factory had opened in the area and they were keen to get involved. So they made up for the shortfall in turkey by handing out half a dozen pair of jeans. We drew lots and, needless to say, I got a pair of frigging jeans. Two sizes too tight for me as well. They always were.

So while the team on the park had moved onwards and upwards the club were stuck in the old days. Amateur in mind, amateur in deed.

Despite it all people now knew of Morton across Scotland, we were competing in the Premier League with Alex Ferguson's developing Aberdeen, Jim McLean's Dundee United and my old team Celtic under big Billy McNeill. Rangers were on the cusp of a decline, but had recently won trebles under Jock Wallace.

And we were doing all this while part-time – one of the few to attempt it at the top level.

I felt we could have won something in the period surrounding that first season in the Premier League. If not the League, then the League Cup or the Scottish Cup, there was certainly a trophy in that team.

For whatever reason it did not happen, be it because we were not good enough or not fit enough – whatever. But at the time we believed there was one trophy in us at least. Especially with the Old Firm at a low ebb.

If you analyse history now it shows that Aberdeen won the League in 1980 and more than once in the years which followed. Dundee United also went on to win the League in 1983 as they formed the so-called 'New Firm'. Maybe we peaked too soon. With an extra push in the right direction I still feel we could have beaten them to the punch.

It was not purely down to Morton, Aberdeen or United raising their standard – though all three clubs most definitely did. There was also a lowering of expectation and achievement at Celtic and Rangers. They had suddenly come back into sight for the rest of us again – particularly Rangers.

Fair play to the New Firm. They had two magnificent managers and produced good, good football teams. They could never hope to be Rangers and Celtic but they peaked at the right time. We did not. We were always punching well above our weight.

We finished that first season in seventh position, but we had been better than that. It was a season of two halves, the first a tale of dazzling excellence, the latter a collective let down caused by a loss of momentum. After starting the season like a train we struggled at the start of 1979 – finally ending that run against Dundee United on 24 March.

But after that we won only three of our last 10 games. By the end people were asking if we were going to survive never mind win the League. But we did – comfortably. For once I was happy to see my boyhood heroes Motherwell go down.

For me personally the season was an unquestionable success. I ended the campaign with 29 goals. And while Dundee United's Paul Hegarty won the Players' Player of the Year on a recount ahead of me, I was recognised by the Scottish Football Writers' Association as the best player in the country.

As I sat down at the top table in the Albany Hotel on 30 April 1979 I was a proud man. A meal of Crème Dubarry, Aiguillette de Boeuf au vin rouge, Haricots verts au beurre followed by Èclair maxime and coffee prepared by a top French chef was somewhat different to my usual standard fare in dietary terms. Yet I only really had only one thing on my mind all night – to make sure my dad always had a bottle of the sponsor's whisky in front of him. It was the least I could do.

Ricky Fulton the comedian was at the top table as a speaker that night. The chairman of Rangers, Rae Simpson spoke, sportswriter Hugh Taylor gave a fine speech and the great and the good of the Scottish game dined at my feet. But the most important men in the room that night were my dad and my grandfather.

The room was bulging with dignitaries but I felt good because Morton people who had never been invited to the dinner in their lives suddenly had a front row table within kicking distance. It changed my life in a sense, raising my profile to a new level.

But I had no need to feel unworthy in any way. I WAS the best player in Scotland that season.

When you had been there week in and week out, scoring the goals and milking the applause you just knew that you deserved this. I did not doubt it.

With respect to Paul Hegarty, a lovely fellow and the man I regarded as my toughest defensive opponent, I should have won the Players' Player as well. But I had too much to say for myself, I upset people.

The sportswriters, of course, like that in a man. They had an overall look at the big picture and recognised that, for once, the best player that season had not been performing at Ibrox or Parkhead – or even Tannadice. The best player had been Andy Ritchie.

My fellow professionals did not agree. I remember hearing I had lost it while doing an interview for STV'S *Scotsport* programme.

I had scored one of my best ever goals for the Scotsport cameras against Partick Thistle at Cappielow.

I dinked in a Brazilian style curling effort inside Alan Rough's right-hand post and big Roughy hadn't an earthly.

I went for a pint after it appeared and it seemed everybody in the country was talking about it. It was beamed across the country thanks to the cameras and they invited me in often for interviews.

This day I was told they were doing a recount and I instinctively knew I had not got it. I was not going to the Players' Dinner anyway, I had not even voted.

Paul had enjoyed a fantastic season, so I had no real qualms over the guy being recognised. I suppose he could just as easily turn around and say it was the 'west coast bias' of the journalists, which landed me the award. But in response to those charges I would say this much. I had not just doubled the gates at Cappielow with my goals, I had tripled them. I was the better player in my opinion that season, scoring goals like they were going out of fashion.

Again, Paul can point to the fact that he was winning international caps I never got. His career was panning out differently from mine.

Despite the fact I was still at Morton, however, I kept one of my mother's old maxims in mind at all times. Like the nose on front of your face it is always in front of you. I believed something would happen for me that summer.

Someone was eventually going to come along and take a chance on me. They had to. There were guys earning big money moves to England at that time I would not have felt in my slipstream as football players.

But this was the pre-Bosman era. People were coming up and asking how they might go about buying me. Hearts, Sheffield Wednesday and Liverpool – Europe's top club at the time – all enquired about me I am told. Every club in England was linked with me. But then Hal would tell them to hand over £1 million and the reaction would always be the same. 'Thanks, but no thanks.' I would not even have paid £1 million for me. For me the worst thing that could have happened began with a phone call from London to Dundee.

The day Raymond Stewart became the most expensive teenager in British football, leaving Dundee United for West Ham for £430,000, was the day the pupils in Hal Stewart's eyes were replaced by pound signs.

Here was a full-back not even 20 leaving Scotland for an English First Division Club for almost half a million quid. Suddenly, Hal's stance on my situation hardened.

When Ray Stewart headed south I was at my peak. I was the Scottish player of the year, I was finding new ways of scoring goals every week and I was hitting them from all angles and distances.

And Hal was quoted soon after as saying, 'how can I sell a guy scoring 30 goals a season to an English club for less than that? This guy can entertain people and score goals. You can buy a full-back anywhere.'

Maybe if he had stuck at £500,000 I might have had a chance. But Trevor Francis had left Birmingham City to go to Nottingham Forest for £1 million that same summer. And with those two transfers my fate was sealed.

There were newspaper articles naming the bright young things in Scottish football, from Aberdeen's Willie Miller, to David Narey of Dundee United and Tony Fitzpatrick of St Mirren. Here was a new generation of Scottish players coming through and guess whose name was always at the top of the list? A certain Andy Ritchie.

When we won promotion a year earlier I had vowed to blank all this talk out, I just wanted to go and score goals and let the rest take care of itself.

There was nothing else I could do. Nowadays you would sit and work out a plan with your agent to weasel your way out of a club by hook or by crook. Or you would patiently wait until the end of your contract and take a Bosman, with a huge signing on fee at the new club of your choice. In those days that was not an option.

There was no freedom of contract, the clubs held the whip hand. The day I signed for Morton in 1976 I effectively signed for life. Or until they decided they had taken all they could from my abilities.

If I became fed up with them it was tough. You want to leave Andy? No can do, unless someone pays up £1 million.

Even if I decided and had enough of it, I was powerless. I could walk out on Morton but I sure as hell was not going anywhere else to play.

Until they decided they wanted to move you on you were their player. It was tantamount to slave labour. We were not quite the modern day equivalent of criminals laying down railroads in America's deep south. But neither were we free to do precisely as we pleased. Not on the park at least. Off it, I was embarking on a perfectly carefree existence.

Chapter Seven

Scotland

MORTON WERE still in the First Division when I first heard the immortal chant, 'Ritchie for Scotland'.

The World Cup was approaching in Argentina and the nation was at fever pitch trying to second guess who the eternally optimistic manager Ally McLeod might take to South America.

Prior to the end of our promotion season in 1977–78 things were going supremely well for me. I was scoring goals, we were winning games, we were upsetting the odds and anything seemed possible. Even the inclusion of a part-time First Division striker in the World Cup squad.

I had played for Scotland's youth team alongside Willie Miller and Jimmy Calderwood of Aberdeen fame, but that had been it. I played in the World Youth Cup while I was on loan at Rob Roy. Jim Blyth, who would play for the full team and go onto assist Gordon Strachan as Celtic goalkeeping coach, was in that youth set up as well.

I also remember playing up front with a fine player called Stevie Finnieston. He would go on to play for Chelsea's first team; but to my knowledge he was never in with a shout of going with the full team to a World Cup Final.

After an unexpected phone call from the Scotland manager Ally McLeod one evening in the middle of 1978, however, it seemed I was.

At that time the window of opportunity for aspiring Scotland internationals was the old Home International Championships. It may be much maligned and little missed now, but the end of season games against Wales, Northern Ireland and especially England were decent occasions then.

For want of a better phrase, I hoped I might somehow sneak up the back steps of the flight to Argentina. I certainly had plenty of people championing me.

First Division players did not play in World Cups. Scotland, remember, was in the midst of a land of plenty where World Class footballers were concerned.

But with all due respect to my international rivals of the period there was not a surplus of star performers in the striking positions.

The squad available to McLeod looked a bit top heavy with strikers who, not to put too fine a point on it, were getting on a bit. So I was always hoping that my chance might crop up.

Times may have changed now; international football might be a poor second relation to the highly paid club environment these days. But then? Playing for your country was the major honour for any aspiring football player.

As my old friend Tommy Burns observed when he was Scotland assistant manager to Berti Vogts, they throw Scotland caps around now like Swizzle sticks. But not in the 1970s.

Dalglish, Jordan, Masson, Rioch, Gemmill et al were top quality players with a proven track record in English and European football. These guys had earned the right to wear a dark blue jersey.

There are fellas coming in to play for Scotland now who get 10, 15 or 20 caps for Scotland then are never seen again. And rightly so. Take a straw poll of older fans and they will tell you that half these guys should never have received one in the first place.

That was not the case when I was banging on the door. The word went out that Ally was looking for someone young to bring in.

You do not go to World Cups with two strikers, you take six. So there was always some grounds for hope.

Not least when Ally phoned me one evening prior to the squad for the Home Internationals being named. If you made that pool of players then you had one foot on the aeroplane to South America. He said to me quite bluntly that he would love to include me in the squad and have me in and around the place.

I had been scoring goals for fun. He asked me how I felt about it and I told him I would not let him down, that I would turn up and do my best if he asked me.

Ally made no bones about it. He told me it was going to be a hard process convincing people that a part-timer playing his trade below the Premier League was worthy of a Scotland jersey – this was unheard of.

But he was looking at what I was doing from set-piece situations as much as anything else. I was making a name for myself with the venom of my free-kicks.

There would always be a premium put on that kind of opportunity in the World Cup because, given the heat and the cultural clash with our group opponents Holland, Peru and Iran the games would inevitably be played at a slower pace.

We would, claimed Ally, need someone in certain circumstances who could come off the bench and get us a goal and I was happy with that. I was never under any illusions that I would be going to keep Dalglish sitting there in the South American heat with his tracksuit top on.

I put the phone down that night and felt a million dollars. After a call like that you start to dream of pulling a blue jersey over your head, of fulfilling the ambitions you harboured as a kid in the school playground in Lanarkshire. I did not sleep a wink.

I remember many years later having a beer with old Ally in Allan McGraw's office at a Morton – Ayr United game. Ally reinvented himself at Ayr in his last major job before retiring and succumbing to the horrible effects of Alzheimer's Disease.

He told me that day that his abiding impression of the phone call to me was of how cocky I had been.

'You kept agreeing with me when I said something positive about you,' said Ally.

'Aye, Ally,' I piped up, 'that's because you were right. That's what was happening at the time. I was a right good player.'

My desire to play for Scotland had heightened four years earlier, during the previous World Cup in West Germany.

Myself and a family friend Bill Johnson had driven all the way over there in his nice new car. This was one hell of a way of breaking it in.

We drove down to Dover, took the car ferry to Calais, and crawled the rest of the way by car.

We lived in a little place called Uber Ursel, 15 miles from Frankfurt, for two games. Then we headed up north to Dortmund for a game as well. There was something in the region of 15,000 to 20,000 Scots over there and the atmosphere before the Brazil game was boisterous. The air was heavy with excitement and expectation. At that time this was all new to Scotland.

In our time near Frankfurt, where fans cavorted in the 'sin strip', decked out in tartan, we watched Brazil train just an hour before our boys at the same centre.

As you did if you were following Scotland we partook of the odd local beer and were lying on the grass sunbathing with our fellow countrymen enjoying the bonhomie.

This was a fantastic experience for me; I was as star struck as the rest of them as Brazil got going. Even their warm-up was a revelation. This was the first time I had ever witnessed the use of the cardboard dummy wall for free-kicks.

Rivelino, the renowned Brazilian set-piece genius, spent the best part of an hour doing nothing other than whacking balls around and over this static wall. I was transfixed; at Celtic we had nothing as brilliantly simple as this and to me it seemed one hell of an idea.

It was not just Rivelino; it seemed to me that half a dozen players were equally adept at free-kicks, midfielders, defenders, strikers, the lot. If the goalkeeper had stepped up and pinged one in the top corner of the net it would not have surprised me one bit.

This was like manna from heaven. A lovely summer's day watching the finest footballers in the world with their socks down to their ankles, nonchalantly training while taking in gallons of water and smiling all the while.

When they were finished we waited for the Scotland bus to appear and it was comical to see the pasty-faced Jocks, some of whom were my more senior Celtic teammates, disembark with woolly jumpers on and their socks tightly wrapped around their shins. Jinky Johnstone and Danny McGrain were there if I recall rightly, following closely in Rivelino's footsteps. It was like turning over the television from Dynasty to Take the High Road; the contrast could hardly be starker.

They did the 20-minute warm-up running around the park and got themselves sweating in their dark, heavy training gear. And it struck me immediately how starkly different this had been from the laid-back samba kings of Brazil.

It made one hell of an impression on me. I had been involved in a few continental international youth team tournaments in Las Palmas and so on. And even the West Germans and the Europeans seemed miles ahead of us in terms of preparation.

They had a much more relaxed atmosphere and whenever you found yourself side by side with a French player or an Italian there was an inferiority complex. In terms of our achievements as a nation we were possibly being too hard on ourselves.

Scotland would qualify for five World Cup Finals in a row after all and European Finals were the norm. Our top players were winning European Cups in Scotland and England, but it never seemed to me that the game in our country was moving with the times.

Whenever I would try the odd fancy flick at Celtic Park, big Jock and Neilly Mochan would bawl out the usual abuse.

'Never mind your fucking flicks Ritchie, any more of that and you'll get a flick up the arse.'

We seemed to think if we tried anything mildly radical that we were being what we might crudely call a 'fanny merchant'.

In the dim, dark Scotland of the 1960s and 70s Ronaldinho would have been classed as being the ultimate waste of space among players and coaches if he had started all that showboating nonsense.

He would not have lasted 10 minutes in Scottish football. And this at a time when Jinky was a Scotland regular. Anyone of my age will nod their head in recollection at that.

When Bill and I got back from Germany I did not exactly revolutionise my training methods in the manner of a man capitalising on a Eureka moment. But I certainly practiced a bit more and tried to bend my free-kicks a little further round a wall.

I tried to see things a new way and watched what people were doing on television that bit closer.

I had always remembered that amazing free-kick worked by Ernie Hunt and Willie Carr at Coventry against Everton in 1970. I was a kid at the time and when Carr flicked the ball up with his heels for Hunt to volley the ball into the net from 25 yards, it took the country by storm. I was always more interested in that kind of goal than the humdrum dross you saw week in and week out.

That was when free-kicks changed. Suddenly they stopped being a simple case of throwing them into the middle and trying to put a head on it.

I worked on them in training and, bit-by-bit, my reputation for hitting them grew. At Morton I was never on Match of the Day or even Sportscene until we reached the Premier League.

But I was garnering some headlines in the papers and by 78 Ally could not miss them.

It was not as if he was saying to me; 'you are going straight into the team, everything will be rosy.'

He wanted to take me along for specific reasons. I scored goals, I was different, I was fresh and I was young. And I took one hell of a free-kick. I wanted this badly. Not least because making the Scotland squad for a World Cup would have gone some way to getting me the move back to the big-time I so craved.

Instead of talking about what I could not do managers might suddenly have started considering what I did bring to the table at the top level.

So I wanted to play against Wales at Hampden in the Home Internationals. If I got a goal against them there then I would have been on my way.

But as time passed I heard nothing else in the days which followed. Eventually word filtered back to me that Ally had encountered some resistance.

It was put to me that certain people at the SFA felt they could not possibly take a part-time player from a part-time club. Ian Archer, a fine sportswriter and broadcaster of his day, was also a friend of mine and a Morton fan and he told me this as we partook of a social refreshment one day in the Kilmacolm Golf Club.

I would not say I spent the weeks before the Home Internationals sitting by a phone. By the time the squad was finally announced word was emerging that big Derek Johnstone of Rangers was likely to get the nod instead.

And he justified his inclusion when he ended up Scotland's top scorer in the Home Internationals with two goals. All of which compounded my distress at being omitted.

If big Derek had come in and had a disastrous Championship I might still have made the plane to Argentina. Ally might have been able to say to the faceless committee men, 'well, look; I've tried the alternatives. I need this boy Ritchie'.

Maybe that was always an act of self-delusion on my part. I was never going to be a vital cog in the wheel; I was only ever likely to be a bit-part player.

I suppose the way things turned out in that particular World Cup I can look now and feel that, in actual fact, I dodged a bullet.

When Willie Johnstone was sent home for failing a drugs test the future Sir Trevor McDonald gave the country back home some shocking news right from the off.

We then lost our first game 3–1 to Peru in disastrous fashion, had an awful 1–1 draw against Iran and then came close to pulling off the impossible dream before falling just short on goal difference after beating the Dutch 3–2 in the final game. That Archie Gemmill scored the most incredible goal ever scored by a Scotland international – and one of the best in World Cup history – was scant consolation.

I would happily have taken all the trials and tribulations of Argentina on my shoulders given half a chance.

It was like most things in life; you never know if the opportunity will ever come round again.

In my case it never did. Scotland returned to the World Cup finals in Spain in 1982 – but by then I was virtually out of football. I was a busted flush. Argentina was my best chance and it slipped past me like a finely streamed Clyde built liner.

And yet to this day I still feel I could have hit a free-kick or two over there. In Argentina the great Mario Kempes was striking them from everywhere, the Dutch were taking turns and the new, much vaunted, leather Tango football had been introduced by Adidas with an adventurous modern design. They were producing these new fangled footballs with triangle designs on them for £50 a time in 1978 and they were like designer items. And when we started using them in the Scottish Premier League the next season I was bending them and curling them like Uri Geller twisting a metal spoon.

I remember thinking when I got my hands on the World Cup balls; 'I could have done something with these. Just one strike, that's all I'd have needed.'

One effort from 30-yards could have put me on the world stage. But, then again, I would still have been a part-time player clubs might have been reluctant to take a gamble on.

If the truth be told, I felt it was my failure to play in the Premier League until the next season which really cost me my place. When Ally McLeod called me and said he faced a battle to get me in there I could hardly disagree. He was right; I had not done anything at the top level in this country other than the odd goal here and there for Celtic in my teenage years.

When Ally's bold 1978 escapade flopped badly that maybe gave me the gee-up I needed; I had told him I could do it and now I had to prove it in the top division with promoted Morton.

Ally's demise as Scotland manager that season was painful, yet inevitable. Rather than seeing it as a door closing at Scotland level I took it as a window of opportunity.

His replacement was the overwhelming fans' choice; Jock Stein, my old Celtic manager.

Jock had left Parkhead after an insulting offer to become a glorified pools manager and had been replaced as manager by Billy McNeill.

Not surprisingly, the greatest manager in Celtic's history had rejected the post and finally taken the plunge into English football.

As Brian Clough had discovered already, however, Leeds United were a poisoned chalice following Don Revie's defection. Homesick, Jock apparently used all his media contacts to get him the national manager's job. In his late 50s he was in the right age range for the post and I hoped his knowledge of what I could do might help me.

It did not quite work out that way as it transpired.

By November 1978 the bandwagon for my inclusion in the national team was gathering unstoppable momentum. I scored a hat-trick for Morton against Dundee United and we were storming towards the summit of the Premier League in our first season with the big boys.

Ian Paul of the *Glasgow Herald* wrote after that game: 'The Morton man really is a phenomenon. At times the watcher has to strain his eyes to find him on the field; at times he is caught in possession like a labouring pensioner; but in between he reveals a bewildering speed of thought, a fascinating audacity and venomous shooting power. He wields a magic influence on all around him at Cappielow, players, bosses and fans.'

After that game our assistant manager Mike Jackson emerged to say: 'There are some people who say he only plays for 20 minutes. But is 20 minutes of that not better than 90 minutes of nothing?' I could not have put it better myself.

Dundee United manager Jim McLean, not given to exorbitant words of praise for anyone, also generously added his voice to the clamour after that game, saying: 'I have never seen a player size up a situation so quickly and execute a move so perfectly.'

Hugh Taylor, a highly respected sportswriter of the time with Glasgow's *Evening Times*, was also trumpeting me for Scotland – yet predicting entirely accurately that my individual streak might work against me: 'Scotland won't be building a team to support Andy. The pattern is set. Today international players fit the style, the style is not built around individuals.'

And yet Hibs manager Eddie Turnbull said encouragingly of my claim; 'He has terrific skills, not far off being a genius.'

And Morton fan and Scotsport presenter Arthur Montford – now a Cappielow director – went so far as to drum up a debate as to whether Ritchie and Dalglish could play together in the same team. It was filling the airwaves and the column inches and, whether he liked it or not, big Jock was under pressure just a month or two into his new job.

But it took time. For the whole of my first season playing in the Premier League he resisted.

Finally, he bowed to the demands and the club informed me they had received a letter from the SFA requesting my release for a European Championship game against Belgium. That was in November 1979 – a full year after the campaign for my inclusion had taken off. There was always an obvious reluctance there.

Hal Stewart told me the news of my call-up verbally and I remember being absolutely ecstatic. By then I had the background of scoring 30-odd goals in the Premier League. I had proved I could do it at that level.

And all I could think at the time was this; if that is what I was doing as a part-time player, what could I do if I ever got the chance to go full-time?

I was told by Hal I would be in the full Scotland squad. Here, at last, was my chance to kick on and improve myself. To show what I could do, not what I could not.

I remember when the full and Under-21 squads were publicly announced it was possibly the first time I had ever paid the slightest attention to them. For once, you see, I was actually involved.

I was in Greenock that day shopping and when someone confirmed to me I was in via the evening paper I could not quite believe what I was reading. I needed a double take.

I was in a Scotland squad alright – but instead of being in the full squad as promised I had been named as the over-age player in the Under-21s.

That was a common consolation prize for the unlucky guy just outside the full set-up at the time. Some prize, some consolation.

I felt sick. But for the fact I was in a shop I would have stood there screaming, cursing and swearing. I will make no bones about this; I was distraught about the whole thing, I simply could not believe it.

I remember thinking big Jock was taking the piss again; the clock was being turned back three or four years to the bitterness of my final days at Celtic.

I was angry and after speaking to friends and family about it I made my mind up; I would withdraw from the squad. I was too old for the Under-21s

– I was 23 for Christ's sake. I was Scotland's Player of the Year, the season's top scorer the season before. What the fuck did I want with the Under-21s? This was adding insult to grave injury.

And then my dad took me aside, sat me down and had a word.

'You go and do what you need to do and play for your country,' he told me. 'It doesn't matter what happens after that, no one can take that away from you.'

It was not so much an act of persuasion as an order. He was telling me not to be so bloody stupid – and he was right.

I did not get Under-21 caps when I was young enough to win them legitimately. Who was I to suddenly think I was too big to be honoured by my country?

And so I flew out as part of the Under-21s with the full squad from Glasgow Airport. The Under-21 game, if I remember rightly, was played in Beveren. And over the course of a three-day trip big Jock did not speak to me; not once.

There was a nod at the start, and as I will explain, a look at the end on the flight home – but that was it.

The coach of the Under-21s was Jim McLean and we had a good team. Alan Brazil was there, a young Gary Gillespie, George McCluskey and a raft of others. We had quite a team. I played alright and after the game we travelled back to Brussels.

Because we were on the same flight as the full squad we watched the game at the Heysel on the Wednesday night before flying home. There was a young guy playing for Belgium that night called Eddy Voordeckers. He gave Scotland a torrid time, scoring the second in a 2–0 win which ended our qualification hopes for the 1980 European Championships. I looked out for him after that. Other than that the memories are scant. Such was my sense of disillusionment with my first experience of playing for Scotland that I had precious little wish to keep a scrapbook of the occasion.

When we flew back on the plane I did not give a toss whether I ever sampled the experience again; I doubted I would.

I remember on that flight home how John Robertson of Nottingham Forest, a flamboyant and superb winger and a European Cup winner that summer, crawled up the plane on his hands and knees to scrounge a fag from me.

In those days smoking on a flight was still permitted and there was I sitting near the front having a cigarette and a bottle of beer. On a Scotland international flight.

Robbo crawled down to me incognito to sneak a smoke because he did not want big Jock to see him smoking and tell Brian Clough. For me this was bizarre; here was a grown man who had been instrumental in bringing Europe's biggest trophy back to his club trying to hide from Jock Stein.

Big Jock glowered at me once, but what did I care? He had only picked me as a token gesture anyway; he was forced into it by outside pressure.

He probably thought to himself that if he played along and isolated me then the clamour would die down and no one would give a stuff. He was right; I was never called up again. I do not think Jock Stein liked being forced into a corner, back against the wall. With that manoeuvre in Belgium, he had put me where he thought I belonged.

In his own book Tommy Burns had told the story of being left out the World Cup in 1982 in fairly brutal fashion. Along with Raymond Stewart, Thomas had been in the provisional squad of 24 prior to the final 22 being named. When big Jock read out his final squad he made no attempt to warn Tommy or Raymond in advance that they were missing the cut.

It was a piece of management, which led Tommy to conclude that Jock could never see him as anything other than 'wee Tommy from the Calton'. He was always the wee guy who had turned up for a reserve game without a coat; the wee fella who was there to sweep the terraces and clean the boots. Familiarity had bred some form of contempt.

Well, I am not sure that applied to me. I think it boiled down simply to the fact that managers like to be the bearers of good news. As soon as it is bad news they are less keen to put their heads over the parapet. The trouble with giving bad news to football players is that you are never entirely sure how they might react; these are confident, fit young men used to being treated like extra special human beings. They do not always take rejection well.

The real strength of an individual lies in how he tells the two who are being left out the squad or the guy being demoted to the Under-21s what is happening to them.

Tommy learned a lesson from his Scotland experience that he carried into his own managerial life. He learned to keep the players on board.

And me? Well I only ever managed at Albion Rovers and it was not for me.

But I was left angry and upset by that experience. I felt Jock Stein had mucked me about in much the same way he had become used to doing at Celtic. I had moved on from the scars of Parkhead by then; I neither wanted nor expected any favours.

But I felt he could have included me in the full squad, as promised at first, and given me a shot. Other people were receiving better treatment at the time. Willie Pettigrew and players like that, without being disrespectful were getting their crack of the whip. Andy Ritchie never got his.

People were telling me it must be personal, that Jock and I did not get on. That was the widespread perception.

But you only endure a poor relationship with someone if you had one in the first place. By the time I left Celtic and knocked on the Scotland door it had been a long time since Jock and I had had any kind of relationship at all. We had nothing to lose and I certainly did not when I had a drink and a fag on the flight home from Belgium.

I tried to adopt a philosophical approach to things thereafter. What was the point of worrying about it?

I had other things to concern me. I was on the verge of overstaying my welcome at Morton.

Chapter Eight

Fame, Fame, Fatal Fame

FOR A time I had been the Player of the Year, man of the moment.

I had gone from being ambling Andy Ritchie, football player, to Andy Ritchie, celebrity. I was being recognised well outwith the boundaries of Greenock. And yet, despite the advertising and appearances and endorsement income coming my way, I was still without a pot to piss in.

My contract was coming to an end and with the vultures hovering, but never quite biting, always being scared away by the price tag. Hal had to do something.

Celtic and Rangers players were earning in the region of £200 a week. When Frank McGarvey, who I topped in the Premier League scoring charts, came back to Celtic from Liverpool he was handed £300 a week to become the club's highest paid player.

At Morton I was one of the country's best players and yet I was on no more than £150 a week – with no discernible means of increasing my footballing income or playing full-time football unless they sold me. And what Morton were saying was that I could go – but only on their exorbitant terms.

Initially I had only bumped up to £50 a week until, at the end of that first contract in 1979, Hal finally honoured his promise to find me a job in order to keep me happy. He made me chief sales agent with the Morton lottery. There would be adverts in the local press urging locals to 'Give Andy a Hand'.

They upped my modest part-time playing salary by around a £100 a week – but that incorporated afternoon work, taking lottery tickets to newsagents and working on the commercial side of the club. That was funded by Ricky Agnew of Agnew Stores. They had also given me £2,000 to sign a new four-year deal.

Financially that was a nice boost. Rena and I bought a new house in Mossend, near Bellshill, from Brian Dempsey. Brian would later go onto become a short-lived Celtic director, a row with Fergus McCann forcing his removal from the board.

At the time he was managing director of Salvesen Homes and he called me up to ask me open the showhouse in Bellshill. As I will explain, my status as Player of the Year in 1979 brought many unexpected invitations and this was one of them.

The homes were worth £25,000 – a king's ransom at the time. And Rena loved them, the soft furnishings and plush shag pile carpets were high fashion. There was cheese and wine and the promise of a new lifestyle. And that day Brian offered to sell me the house next door, fully fitted out with white goods and carpets and curtains for a discounted price.

I then organised for Gordon Strachan and Mark McGhee, who had by now moved up to the North East, to open Brian's other showhome in Aberdeen. If they also made a purchase then they surely held onto it longer than me. With a little more cash in my pocket I was gambling more. Soon enough we had to sell the house and move back in with my mother-in-law to pay off my debts.

For a time, however, the champagne flowed. I was flavour of the month, the summer golden boy. I felt like a big fish. Barratt Homes arranged one of their trademark helicopters to do an opening for them as well.

Suddenly I was playing darts with Jocky Wilson on television at the invitation of Tennent Caledonian Breweries. I was doing celebrity appearances and I was opening this, that and the next thing.

Alexander's the Ford dealers in Greenock, were giving me top of the range cars to drive around in. Sam Torrance, the promising young Largs golfer and future Ryder Cup winning captain also had one as I recall. In return I would pose for a picture, with the headline reading, 'Andy Ritchie Scores with Ford', or some other clichéd nonsense.

The benefits were great. I was being given free wheels, while Tennent's had me touring their free houses where I could drink even more of their beer.

I made acquaintances rather than friends in that period. People were coming out of the woodwork, but I was not David Beckham exactly. I know the modern-day player feels it essential to have an entourage – I did not.

I did not need a support network, I was becoming carried away by my own waves of publicity. Show me someone modestly well known who has not gone that way. You are introduced to this lifestyle so diverse from your own humble beginnings and it goes to your head. Or what is left of it after all the free beer has gone down the hatch.

All of a sudden this new lifestyle was intruding on my preparations for a new season. But the money was never especially great at Morton so why should I not take my chance to grab a slice of the good times?

I was being recognised wherever I went. The most bizarre example of which actually came in the 1980–81 season, a year or so after the mayhem had reached its peak. Morton had entered the old Anglo-Scottish Cup, a half-baked attempt at a British Cup. It was a nice idea, but doomed to failure.

We were drawn against Notts County, a decent team at the time.

And I remember lying in my room in the Central Hotel in Nottingham waiting for the game that afternoon when I took a call from a friend of mine by the name of Bobby Galbraith.

He came from Bellshill but had moved to the Nottingham area many years previous to this call. I thought it was the usual; an old buddy crawling out the woodwork in the search for a match ticket.

'Andy, how are you?' he asks, all raised voice and bonhomie.

'Bobby,' I replied, awaiting the inevitable request for a favour. 'I am in my bed waiting for the game.'

'Aye, sorry, I will not keep you. What you doing after the game?'

Now he was talking my language. We were staying down there after the match and travelling back up the next morning. If Bobby wanted to come round for a beer or something to eat then great. In those days I was always feeling sociable.

'I am bringing a pal with me Andy, he wants to meet you.'

'Not a problem, Bobby, I will get you a couple of tickets sorted out for the game and then I will see you back here.'

So we played the game and I was having one of those wild and wonderful evenings I seemed to specialise in at that time. Everything was coming off for me, every flick, every pass – though we eventually went out 3–1 on aggregate in the quarter-finals.

Afterwards I showered and changed and went to meet Bobby at the main reception where this guy was standing beside him with crepe soled shoes, luminous socks, a long teddy boy jacket and a frilly shirt with a bootlace tie.

It was Dave Bartram, the lead singer of Showwaddywaddy, a popular band of the time who seemed to have spent every week in the Top Ten at the end of the 70s. Dave was Bobby's pal and was desperate to meet me.

I struggled to get my head round this. Alright, the guy was not Rod Stewart or Bowie and his band were not maybe the most fashionable of rock acts, but this fella was never off *Top of the Pops*. In 1979 they were big-time. A band of teddy boys, Showwaddywaddy racked up 10 Top Ten hits in the 70s and 80s and were staples of Saturday night television. And yet here was the lead singer standing waiting to meet me like a smitten autograph hunter. I felt it should have been the other way round.

We drove from Nottingham to Leicester to get a curry, had a drink, had a laugh and – as was now becoming obligatory on these occasions – smoked a bit of dope.

Eventually Dave took me back to the team hotel at 6am. It would be the one and only time I ever met him, but we had a great night and he was all over me like a cheap suit. He told me how he had heard all about my reputation up the road and had seen my goals and read all about me. And as this pop star told me all this I remember thinking to myself, 'you have cracked it now big boy!'

If the truth be told I was living the life of a minor rock star for a year or so, but I had never really thought of it in those terms until that night. The biggest problem was that I had no means to support my increasingly wayward lifestyle. I could – and should – have cleaned up when I was still hot. But, as you do, I thought it would last forever.

The father of Radio Clyde DJ George Bowie, an impresario and promoter, had contacted me in 1978 about some showbiz work. He had entertainers like the comedian Andy Cameron and Mr Abie on his books and all sorts of folk who would fill the bill at Glasgow's Pavilion Theatre.

But I came from a background where that kind of thing was regarded as a bit affected. I did not want to end up being thrust forward as some kind of poor man's Des O'Connor. My interests never lay in being ordered to do things, which would deprive me of my dignity. I was quite capable of doing that by myself, thanks.

But football was evolving. The Winter of Discontent might have witnessed the army collecting the rubbish piled up on the streets, and unions running the country but there were still shafts of light for the professional footballer. People on the make were seeking out new ways to eke money from footballers beyond an ability to kick a ball.

Usually that only went as far as the Scottish Cup Final captains appearing on Glenn Michael's *Cartoon Cavalcade* on STV once a year.

But eventually I agreed to put a toe in and test the water. I took on the odd gig or two when I was 'hot' in publicity terms. Red Rum, the legendary racehorse and Grand National institution, came up to officially open the Tote Bookmakers in Port Glasgow and Greenock. For winning the National three times the horse's owners were being paid £500 appearance money. I was getting £400 for appearing alongside – three times my weekly wage at the time.

I also kicked off the Billy Smart Circus at the Kelvin Hall in 1979. I was playing football with a performing elephant at one point.

The BBC, to my shame, were there to film it. One of their producers, a friend of mine by the name of Jim Hossack, sent over a crew to get the event on tape for posterity. Oddly enough, I have never sought out a video to reminisce. Another thing I took on was when well-known local DJ, 'Tiger' Tim Stevens, and me would go to local schools where he would play music and I would tell the kids how to behave. At the time, however, I am not entirely certain I was the best example to anyone on that score.

For all these new fangled showbiz ventures I was still of the old school of players who enjoyed a Sunday afternoon bevvy session before moving on to the working men's clubs of Lanarkshire.

I liked the odd Wednesday, Thursday or Friday night out as well. My only rule was that the day had to have a 'y' in it. Then it was fair game for another Tennent's event or a more private affair in a howff of my choice.

When you are young you think you can tackle the world and cock a snook at responsibility. When people with large expense accounts and advertising budgets are filling your head full of nonsense that is doubly true.

Somehow or other I was getting away with it because I was still able to produce some magic on the football pitch on a Saturday. I was covering up a multitude of sins.

Some might say that I squandered or wasted my money. But when they say that now I am reminded of the old George Best tale where a porter walks into a five star hotel room to find this footballing legend half naked on the bed beside Miss World, with a couple of bottles of champagne by his side and bundles of freshly printed banknotes all around them.

The porter walks in, sighs, and asks: 'where did it all go wrong George?'

Well I never had any Miss Worlds, not even a Miss Bellshill. I drank Guinness and spirits and I certainly never had much money. But to me those days and nights of hedonism never felt wrong at the time. If they had I would have stopped doing them.

Morton were going well and I wanted to show I was the jewel in the crown.

The 60s and 70s players maybe went so far as to present a trophy to the winner of the two o'clock race at Hamilton Racecourse in return for a lovely day out. They would only participate further by gambling or drinking.

By 1979 I was opening the bloody meeting. There was a lot happening and it was new and it was fresh. The game was changing and I was a pioneer for the new cult of the celebrity footballer. There was no template to say, 'this is how you do things'.

It had never happened before. Footballers had not been asked to lead Red Rum into bookmakers' shops before. These days Ally McCoist and Gary Lineker can be television personalities – in those days that was unheard of. Footballers were footballers and that was that.

But when I pan back now and reflect on the humiliation of playing football with elephants for 10-year-old kids I take one thing from it above everything else; I did not take myself too seriously.

Jim Hossack told me years later that was why he took to me. There were footballers then – and there certainly are now – who are so far up their own arses they could taste their toenails. I was never one of those guys.

These days the monetary lunacy of modern football makes players aloof, these guys have lost the plot. They are so well paid they can no longer relate to the people who pay their wages.

That was never me. Even when I had my 15 minutes of fame you would still find me standing in the pub with my mates laughing and enjoying the company. A roped off area in some dark nightclub where they charge you £20 to hang up your coat was never my scene.

Sure, I took some stick the day after my elephant kick-about appeared on national television. But I walked through the dressing room door and took the abuse before returning it with interest. I never lost my conceit of myself as a footballer; I had an attitude when it came to management and authority. But when it came to dealing with supporters and so on I was always accessible, I never got above myself there.

Getting a bigger head than I already had was never likely to be a problem. It was other areas – specifically my waistline – which concerned Morton most.

Chapter Nine

Kidnapped

MORTON's second season in the Premier League was hurtling ever closer when I was effectively kidnapped.

I was reluctantly cajoled into a fast car at 8am on a Sunday morning and driven south, largely against my will.

Morton chairman Hal Stewart was my abductor, driving me to the select Stobo Castle Spa in Peebles and dumping me on the driveway with a suitcase just after 11am. It was, he insisted, for my own good. It hardly needed saying that it was very much in Morton's interests as well.

I tend to describe the period, which followed my Player of the Year award as my Smirnoff Summer. I was drinking faster than they could rack up the pints on the bar. And by the time pre-season started I had forgotten when to stop.

I would roll up for training on a Tuesday night reeking of booze then disappear into a haze of alcoholic hedonism for two days until the next session on the Thursday night. To say I was not exactly preparing like a monk for the new season with lengthy periods of contemplation and prayer would be putting it lightly. And neither was I doing anything likely to help me lose weight. My contribution to shifting the pounds was to replace food with liquid lunches – and you do not see that recommended on the WeightWatchers programme too often.

As a result I had ballooned up to 16 and a half stones by the time pre-season weigh-ins were taken.

When I was informed of my burgeoning frame with a gasp I was less surprised. I had a fair idea of my spreading girth. How could it be otherwise when I had spent the entire 10 weeks of rest working my right elbow hard in every pub I could find?

As a result Morton decided drastic action was needed. We were due to start the new season against Celtic at Parkhead and, as the star player, something had to be done to save me from myself and get me in shape. They clearly felt I could not be trusted under my own steam. Quite rightly so.

And so I was smuggled off to Stobo Castle early one morning. It was a plush baronial era retreat for the rich and famous close to Peebles in the Scottish borders. I was booked in for three weeks, during which time I was discharged only briefly for the opening League game at Celtic Park. The idea was simple; to get the pounds off me and get me back to my fighting weight for the battles ahead.

We had played Berwick Rangers in a League Cup section game, the traditional curtain raiser for the new season at that time.

And despite being in training for three weeks solid I could not lose a pound due to my extra-curricular activities – and against Berwick it showed.

After that game Hal came the next day to drive me to my secret hideaway. I always thought that when the men came to take me away they would be wearing white coats. I do not rightly recall how Hal was dressed, but me carrying on the way I was threatened to turn his complexion a whiter shade of pale. This was me embarking upon the early footballing equivalent of rehab.

When I was dumped on the doorstep with a warning to get fit in two weeks I thought I was going to jail, but it was one hell of an incarceration.

Hal had left me in the care of a lovely family called the Wynyards. Steven and his mother ran the place and they could not possibly have treated me any better.

I had two weeks to get in shape before the Celtic opener and I was in distinguished company. Lulu, the Glaswegian singer with a string of hits to her name, was staying there at the time. And so was Joan Collins, in her pre-Dynasty years, with her husband Ron Kass, the president of Apple Records during the heyday of the Beatles.

So none of these people were exactly poor. Which consequently meant the place was not exactly cheap. This was clearly costing Hal Stewart and Morton an arm and a leg.

For a fortnight I did nothing but diet and undergo spa treatments.

I had to lose 18 pounds in that period – that was my minimum target.

It could not have been costing Stobo Castle much to feed me. If I ate much more than a leaf of lettuce for my evening dinner on any given night that was a rarity. But they were providing me with a top class physiotherapist and trainer, not to mention a string of specialists in chiropractic advances and so on. This was a serious health farm.

The German physio had been a champion sprinter at Powderhall, the annual 110 metre dash held at the old Edinburgh greyhound venue until 1999. He would hammer me every afternoon and evening in training and see to it that I dieted and had all the appropriate treatments. From Jacuzzis to foot scrubs, I had the lot. In comparison with pre-season training this was a blast.

Not least given the presence of the late, great Jimmy Steele as a fellow guest. To the uninitiated Jimmy had been a legendary masseur at Celtic Park under big Jock and as luck would have it he was there to provide some companionship for yours truly. To say Steely was a character would be putting it mildly.

I had a bit of a back problem at the time and he would have me roaring and laughing as I lay having the seaweed treatment, wrapped tightly in hot towels.

It was not all pleasure, by God there were torturously hard days of work as well. They were not messing about – Hal would not have let them. He was paying a fortune for this after all.

But we had fun along the way. There were a party of Saudi Arabian airline hostesses and myself and Steely would josh along with them of an evening.

Lulu would keep her distance during her stay – but, in common with most Scots at the time, knew who I was.

I used to open doors in the morning when I saw her and start belting out my own rendition of Shout – her best-known hit. I might have been hanging around with pop stars, but that episode proved I was never likely to make the bill on Top of the Pops anytime soon.

Steven Wynyard was very indulgent at the time. He reminded me slightly of Jason King, the suave hero of the early 70s cult television programme Department S. He would have the suits and big collars and he and his mother ran the place.

If I threw a pair of underpants down they would be returned to me washed and ironed before they hit the floor.

The Wynyards would also grant me the use of a car to drive into Peebles. I was not allowed to go into pubs or drink alcohol.

And that was the key to the pounds dropping off. As with so many things I was misunderstood on that score.

People always cracked the 'Andy Ritchie ate all the pies' gag.

But it may surprise people to know that eating was never my vice. It was booze, which made me bloated and heavy; food rarely got a look-in.

I had been on what might best be described as a bender that summer. I went on holiday a few times and spent some time down at a caravan in Girvan on the Ayrshire coast we would use from time to time. All the while I was drinking heavily.

Sure, I would eat Chinese takeaways and so on – and that did not help. But to say that was the source of my physical malaise would be untrue. Maybe Rena could have exerted more influence, but she was not with me most of the time. I would be leaving Mrs Ritchie in the house to look after the boys while I went out to enjoy myself.

Whenever there was a day out big Andy was there. And the days out invariably turned to nights out as well. Sometimes even overnights.

It was not difficult because I am not boasting when I say that there were no lack of invites.

The word would go out that Andy Ritchie was coming along to a session and suddenly folk would be on the phone. And their friends would quickly be there to be in my company. And they would want to buy me a drink as well; I was never likely to stop them.

So Hal was left with no choice but to take drastic action; however costly. The price of failing to sort me out might have been Morton's place in the Premier League. And that was worth more than a fortnight in a health spa, however exclusive.

I got over the shock of being driven to Stobo as soon I saw how luxurious the place was. It was in keeping with my new celebrity status; I just accepted it as part and parcel of a great big game.

At the time I was never as serious as I am now. To me staying in five star accommodation with international stars was an adventure, an experience to be savoured.

It was at Stobo that the first famous Andy Ritchie perm came into being. Me and Steely would entertain some of the beauty therapists in Peebles and the reward would be streaks in the hair and a well-manicured moustache.

I had hours to kill during the day between physio sessions or between a steam bath and a sauna. So I would go along and the girls would do your hair, darken your sideburns or give you deep cleansing skin treatment; you name it they did it. Aromatherapy featured as well as I recall.

And when that was done I would collect a gun and go and shoot rabbits in Steven's grounds. I was living the life of a country squire. Some might have seen that as me being Billy big-time. I did not – I just saw it as passing time.

I fell just short of my original target for weight loss after the first two weeks. But Stobo Castle worked, in so much as I lost 17 pounds and returned to Cappielow in time to face the champions at Parkhead, my old pal Tommy Burns on the other team.

I scored twice that day in a 3–2 defeat despite failing to train once with my teammates in the two weeks prior to the game.

They looked at me when I walked into the dressing room as if I was ill. It was described to me as being not dissimilar to looking at a stricken sole with a terminal illness. I looked gaunt compared to the bloated character who had gone down to Stobo a fortnight earlier.

The truth is that I should have scored a hat-trick at Parkhead. I had a golden chance to grab us a draw and a morale boosting point on the opening day. I blew it, but still I was heartened by my performance.

To celebrate my freedom I had a couple of glasses of red wine and a steak and salad in an Italian restaurant in Glasgow that night before being whisked back to Stobo Castle in Hal's car once more to finish my course.

I was back there for another three or four days until the 18th pound came off and then my course was finished and I was free to go.

Did it change me? Did it make me see the error of my ways or rethink my lifestyle? Did it hell.

After all I had scored twice against Celtic and had shrugged off the weight-gain. And If I had done that once I could do it again. Why should I change the way I go about my everyday lifestyle? I was enjoying myself fine and scoring goals thanks.

The club had solved my problems. I had been a stone and a half overweight and they had been desperate enough to send me away to a lovely retreat to get it off. And if they were that desperate once, they would surely do the same the next time as well. I had learned nothing.

I went back to my old ways and I was not especially choosy over my choice of tipple. It was whatever you wanted in essence.

Beer, vodka, whisky; rack it up and I would drink it. It was not a case of needing to down a bottle at 10am in the morning to get through the day. I was never in that kind of trough. But the sociable drinking was out of control.

I liked my beer and lager, my Tennent's Special. Most of it laid on by my sponsors free of charge.

The beer was for early on in the evening and then, when I began to feel bagged up; I would switch to whisky and spirits.

At no point did I begin to reflect on the fact that I might have a problem with alcohol. At that time Alcoholics Anonymous and other help groups were regarded as concept movements; airy-fairy talking shops for sandal wearers and oddballs.

There was no deep lying psychological reason for my activities. I could not point to some awful episode in my life and break down in tears by way of an explanation.

I just drunk too much because I enjoyed it, it was that simple.

The circumstances of the time were that I was in demand for nights out and there were people more than happy to give me the booze for nothing just to have Andy Ritchie drinking their product. Which I was more than happy to help them with.

It was not just sponsors. To this day I can walk into a hostelry in downtown Greenock, three decades years since I became the finest player in the club's modern history, and keep my hands buried deep in my pockets.

I could take you to the Wetherspoons pub close to the central train station right now and my money would be superfluous. And it is not only there by any means. In Slainte bar in Nicholson Street they have an Andy Ritchie Travel Club.

The Spinnaker Bar and Hotel in Gourock also has its own Morton Supporters' bus running every weekend and I can still recall the first time I drank in there.

My ex-wife and I stopped by there a few years ago, long after I had ceased to play for Morton, on a beautiful summer's night.

I walked up to the bar for a round of drinks and asked for a couple of Bacardis and coke in long glasses with plenty of ice. And the owner Stuart McCartney, now a good friend of mine, took one look at me and said; 'Your money's no good in here.'

For a minute I was concerned. This guy was clearly a St Mirren or a Rangers fan with a long memory or he bore some form of strange grudge. It soon became apparent though that Stuart was a Morton diehard taking the chance to repay me for being the best player he had ever witnessed at Cappielow.

And if that is the case now then I can only describe the situation in 1979 as being 100 times worse. Or better depending on your perspective. At that time my popularity was not just confined merely to Inverclyde and its delightful backstreets.

I could go anywhere and expect to be bought drinks. I was lording it free of charge in towns and villages as diverse as Stonehaven and Laurencekirk in Aberdeenshire. Had I gone to the Western Isles or Orkney the result might have been the same there as well.

I did not have a preferred boozer as such in that long summer of 79. It would be suffice to say that I hung out wherever the mood took me.

I did not particularly enjoy Glasgow, that was too busy and people were too in your face and aggressive. Tommy Burns once observed that half of Glasgow hates you and the other thinks it owns you when you have an Old Firm connection. And he had a point. It would invariably be more familiar breeding grounds such as Hamilton and Motherwell for me.

I never went out looking for trouble, so I was never likely to attract the attention of the newspapers. Though, if I found it, the culture of the tabloids was different then; less invasive. The sportswriters earned more than we did; we had a cosier relationship than they do with the highly paid, aloof modern player.

Wherever I went there would be occasional times when familiarity bred contempt and people would say things to me I did not particularly want to hear.

'You should not be out drinking before a game,' became the words I despised more than anything else. Nosey bar stewards with nothing better to fill their miserable lives would hit me with moral lectures, while sitting there with bulbous noses glowing like the Millennium Dome.

'Do you not think you should be training harder and drinking less?' was usually the follow-up. And they were right. But I did not want to hear it.

I would be prone to asking what the fuck they knew about it? How many goals had they scored in the Premier League? I had scored 22 the season before while behaving like this. What about them?

There were times when I could be an aggressive, fighting drunk or – more commonly – everybody's pal. Some might say I was in denial concerning my behaviour. I would be more inclined to call it arrogance; a belief that I could self implode and dodge the consequences. I thought I was indestructible.

And when I had a good drink the other vices inevitably followed. I was always a smoker and marijuana was readily available to me.

I used to enjoy a smoke after the game, coming back down with a joint of ganja. And, it would be true to say that I occasionally had a smoke on a Friday night as well.

I do not think I would have passed many compulsory post-match drugs tests at that time, let's put it that way. I was fortunate they never did them. I could resist virtually everything but temptation. I hadn't been brought up in a way, which would equip me to deal with the sudden attention.

The drinking also diminished my inhibitions when it came to gambling. I do not like to gamble when I am drunk – but I am more likely to do it.

I had not been in a showbiz family; I had not been a singer or an actor. I was introduced to this lifestyle purely because I was doing reasonably well as a footballer with Morton.

I scored plenty of goals in 1979–80 and felt fit – but by the end of the season I was probably back up to 16 stone again.

It was life's rich tapestry. I just kept thinking, 'I will go back to Stobo next season. Morton will pay.'

I do not remember any alarm bells ringing or thinking I had to do something. But then, if truth be told, I do not remember a great deal at all about that period.

Like anybody I did a lot of waking up in the morning wishing I had behaved differently the night before. I had a young family, but the trouble was that I always convinced myself there was nothing inherently wrong with the way I was behaving. It was almost as if I felt the need to cancel out every good act on a football pitch with something bad off it.

I was scoring goals, but inevitably I knew in my heart of hearts I was not playing as well as the season wore on. The priority became less one of playing well and more a case of doing enough to get by. To hang on in there.

Morton were doing likewise. We ended 1979–80 in sixth place and I had scored 19 League goals, 27 in all competitions. In the Premier League only Doug Somner of St Mirren scored more than me.

We also reached the League Cup semi-final where we met the eventual champions Aberdeen. The Dons were a team on the make, being forged skilfully by Alex Ferguson. But we had the hex over them for much of the season, beating them three out of four times – including a game in November 1979 at Pittodrie where I scored a late winner in a 2–1 comeback victory.

In the semi-final we prepared confidently enough, but we just froze, it was as simple as that.

Our proximity to a major trophy terrified some of the team and the game was over before it began. We did not do ourselves justice.

We finished sixth in the League – one place better than our inaugural campaign. But I cannot deny that I was feeling more and more strongly that I should be getting my move. A move I had been promised countless times, but ultimately denied.

I had overachieved on the football pitch but had been underpaid off it. The lack of full-time football was leading me down the wrong path.

One or two of the other boys were moving on, Jim Tolmie to Lokeren in Belgium, Neil Orr going to West Ham and Bobby Thomson to Middlesbrough – while I was stuck going nowhere.

I didn't want to be hanging around beyond that second season in the Premier League going round the same old merry-go-round of Ibrox, Parkhead and long trips to Pittodrie. Twice a season we would go to these places and play the teams concerned four times in all. More if we also drew them in the Cup competitions.

I had scored 100 goals and more for Morton when Jock Stein's parting phrase began to come back to me.

I could not get a move and I was sinking deeper and deeper into what the big man had called the elephant's graveyard. I was in trouble.

Suddenly there was a realisation that this was not going to happen for me, that my window of opportunity had passed me by.

It was a very small space of time between me thinking I was going places to the realisation that I was in fact going nowhere.

As players left, Morton were sliding a little bit further back with every season.

Yet in 1980–81 we made it to the Scottish Cup semi-final – and here, after our League Cup semi disappointment of the previous season, was our big chance of silverware.

There had been some measure of revenge for that defeat in the fourth round of the Cup when we defeated Aberdeen at Cappielow. Pictures of that game show me scoring one of my best ever goals, turning Willie Miller and Alex McLeish – Scotland's central defensive partnership – this way and that before chipping the ball into the net beyond Jim Leighton in goal. Aberdeen would not lose another Scottish Cup game for some time after that. So when we made it to the last four we were entitled to fancy our chances.

I remember us going to Largs a few days before the big game to prepare and escape the clamour for tickets. It had not, in truth, been a great season. I had been up and down, performing at certain times and not at all at others.

If I am being blunt then I have to admit that I kept my best performances for the television cameras coming. Unlike now there was no blanket coverage. They picked one game to highlight on Saturday night and that was it.

My drinking and gambling was as bad as ever. But I always seemed to be able to produce a big performance when the stakes were high, for all that my goal tally would drop to a disappointing 11 for the season – the first time I had fallen below 20 in a Morton shirt.

The semi-final stage at Hampden against an indifferent Rangers team managed by John Greig was tailor-made for me. I thought and assumed I would be playing. When we came back to Greenock on the Friday, 24 hours before kick-off, I remember we headed to Cappielow for a final training session.

And down at the far side before the wee Dublin end, as they called one of the terraces at the old place, wee Benny called me over for a word.

'You're not playing,' were his exact words to me.

I thought I had misheard.

I thought he was taking the piss. 'You're what?' I asked.

'I'm not going to play you,' he repeated for clarity. 'You're not playing, I'm leaving you out and you're on the bench.'

Because the rest of the boys were there I went back to training and decided against a scene.

But when I travelled home in a black daze I told Rena and she was as disbelieving as me.

None of us could take it in. Somehow I felt that he would see sense, that I would get the call in the morning and everything would be okay. I would start the game, I believed. I was fooling myself.

He was, I believed, trying to provoke a reaction; trying to make me wake from my complacent slumber and pull the finger out. I went to bed convinced it was a managerial masterstroke to make big Andy a Cup hero.

But it was not. I got to Celtic Park where the semi-final was being played and nothing had changed. I was out.

I felt like some form of pariah. It was as if no one could look at me, I had been drummed out the inner sanctum.

In a moment of self-reflection before the game I thought to myself that, even though I had not always been fair with Benny, even though I had been a complete prick, this was unforgiveable.

How could he forget where we had come from? When I arrived Morton were second bottom of the First Division. I had averaged 27 goals per annum over four years and yet it had come to this.

Eventually I came off the bench and at 2–0 down we got a penalty which I converted. And we were unlucky not to get a replay. We were down to nine men due to some erratic refereeing and we had a goal chalked off. I remember a couple of chances and we pushed them all the way towards the end.

And I knew as we pressed that if we got a second game he would fucking well play me then and, by God, I would show him. I would win the fucking Cup for Morton.

But it was not to be. We lost the semi-final, Rangers reached the Final and our relationship had changed forever. There was no way back.

I have no idea why Benny did it. He said at the time he wanted a more physical edge to our play and as time goes on he will probably tell people that he left me out for this reason or that reason. In Morton Greats by Graeme Ross Benny had this to say: 'It was one of the hardest decisions that I ever had to make in football. It's easy to say in hindsight that I should have played Andy, but I knew it would be a physical match and decided to bring in a different type of player. But I made the decision at the time and you live or die by it.'

The bottom line was that he felt I was not doing enough. And if he had just come to me and said that man to man, we could have discussed it. How do you get to a semi-final of the Scottish Cup if your key players are not doing enough? You have to win three matches to get there. I had won us the game against Aberdeen. And yet, in my heart of hearts, I knew that the real problem lay with me and not Benny. I had problems I was not facing up to.

Benny would not have left me out the team if I had been behaving myself and playing well every week.

When I look back on it now there is no room for doubt. I was doing neither. But on that day, in that place, in that moment when he told me I was out, my Morton career was effectively over.

Chapter Ten

A New Start

I ALWAYS knew where I stood with Jock Wallace.

In the summer of 1983 I finally earned my release warrant from Morton to join Motherwell, where this gruff, former Malaysian jungle fighter ruled the roost.

Unlike his former Old Firm rival Jock Stein, Wallace never played games, never messed me around. I knew precisely where I stood and I liked it.

On the face of it Jock was as straightforward as they came. Physically he would stand there and fight you without blinking. He'd land a right hook first and think second. Yet, he also had a softer side few ever truly witnessed. He was a real man's man. He would have a drink with you and tell you precisely what was on his mind. Sometimes in the most unexpected fashion as I quickly discovered.

I remember a pre-season game up north against a Highland League team. I played half an hour and was at the bar having a shandy with my teammate, Motherwell left-back Ian McLeod.

Suddenly big Jock swept in, craned around the room and spotted my drinking buddy.

'You were hopeless tonight son,' he said, with nothing by way of a greeting or a handshake.

Then, with the minimum of backlift, Jock stuck the head in him. Just like that. Call it a Glasgow kiss, a headbutt, a stookie, whatever you like. Either way it was a hell of a blow straight to the bridge of McLeod's nose.

I had been at the club just four weeks and had never witnessed anything like it in my life.

I checked if Ian was alright and as he raised his head, hand over a reddened, swollen nose, he looked unshaken.

'Ach, he's done it before,' he told me. And we drank on as if nothing had happened.

I resolved there and then that if Jock ever tried anything of the like with me then he would have his violence returned – with interest. Thankfully, we never did, our relationship proved short if not altogether sweet.

The move to Motherwell came about when I was on a family holiday with Rena and the boys in Germany.

Jock called my home in my absence and left a message with my mother-in-law. If I fancied a move to Motherwell I should phone him as soon as possible on my return.

I eventually caught him as he was heading off to Spain, where he was having a holiday home built near Seville. In time Jock would enjoy a brief spell as coach of the Spanish giants, but at this point he was the humble manager at Fir Park. Wallace had made his name as a coach at Rangers before ending the nine-in-a-row dominance of Scottish football's other colossal Jock, of the Parkhead vintage.

In 1975–76 and 77–78 he actually led Rangers to the domestic treble before leaving in mysterious circumstances for Leicester City, where he won the old Second Division and reached the semi-finals of the FA Cup. For Motherwell, luring him back to Scotland was quite a coup.

The saga of my transfer went on for four weeks, in my mind becoming a rival to J.R. Ewings run-ins on Saturday night TV in *Dallas*. Jock would call me regularly to tell me Morton were putting all kind of obstacles in the way of a deal.

I would later discover there had been a reason for that; they did not want it getting out that I was leaving for another club until they had sold a respectable number of season tickets.

When I finally did leave for the Steelmen, it should have been a dream come true. Here were my boyhood team finally giving me the chance to walk through the Fir Park doors as a home player. Things went sour so quickly there, however, that I was quickly wishing I had stayed at Morton.

And given how things had degenerated at Cappielow that was saying quite something.

I should have left Greenock when I was hot, when I was Player of the Year and scoring goals in 1979. If not precisely at that time, then soon afterwards. For the last two or three years I was festering and becoming stale. I was still training just two nights a week and in professional football terms I was skimming around the edges.

There had been a window of opportunity, which had closed. It was as if my 15 minutes of fame had passed. And suddenly I was struggling. I was not alone but I felt as if I might as well be.

All around me Morton were selling their best players. My failure to win a move was becoming more and more conspicuous and the guys coming in alongside me were of a lesser quality. In Premier League terms we had punched above our weight long enough; there was a reckoning in the air.

We had lasted five seasons at the top level but after three I had passed my peak. So had Morton. The Cup semi-final and my omission, in 1981, had been the beginning of the long goodbye. I should have been gone before that; maybe if I had left then I might have salvaged a career elsewhere. I had only managed 11 goals that season, but in the four previous campaigns I had averaged close to the 30 mark. Something was clearly going wrong, but I felt someone else should be fixing it, not me.

New guys were coming in to replace the Bobby Thomsons, Jim Tolmies and Neil Orrs; men who had played no part in getting us to the Premier League. And they would be the same guys who would be instrumental in taking us back down again.

And yet at this point I should put down the stone and step away from the glasshouse. When Morton were put in their place and relegated back to the First Division in 1982–83 – my final season – I had downed the tools. If truth be told, I did not give a damn by then whether I played or not. Morton could go hang.

Attitudes were changing towards me. Where before my behaviour was tolerated because I was scoring all these goals, now there were no grounds for indulgence. Benny Rooney and Mike Jackson, his assistant, were growing more pissed off with me by the week.

They would leave me out the team, we would argue, we would play games with each other. Much of my respect and affection for Benny had gone that day at Cappielow when he told me I would not play against Rangers in the semi. From then on it was a downward spiral.

From two guys who used to stand talking football outside his wife's hairdresser's in Cambuslang before my move to Morton, we were now virtual strangers.

From this distance people might think I overreacted to that, that I should have knuckled down. But I had been key to getting Morton to the semi-finals in the first place and I was desperate to play in a final at Hampden. I felt betrayed and I could never quite shake that off.

My game had always been based around confidence. You have to be up to the mark and have your eye on the ball. Take your eye off the ball and the goals dry up.

I had lost that fire I had in my belly when I was scoring.

The young man who had gone to bed at 10pm in Montrose as my errant teammates hit the town in my early months at the club had left the building. Now I was one of them, a wizened, wayward, kindred spirit.

I could not shake the same feeling every day; I had scored 30 goals then I would score another 30 goals then another 30 goals – and I was STILL there. How many more fucking goals would I need to score to get the move I craved?

And Benny or someone else would say to me, 'ah, but it's not all about goals, it's about doing this or that as well.'

It was always about something else; it was always 'you don't do this, you don't do that'.

What no one ever seemed to notice was what I DID do. And that was put the ball in the back of the net; football's most important art.

Luther Blissett was at unfashionable Watford at that time, scored goals for fun and won himself a £1 million move to AC Milan. He was never what you might call a technically gifted player. I scored one of my best ever goals against him and Graham Taylor in a pre-season game – a 40-yard howitzer.

But Blissett got his move because he scored a lot of goals for Watford as they rose up through the ranks. He was back within a year for half the price, but to me that did not matter. I suppose what he had in his favour was the recognition of his country – England capped him 14 times.

But was he a better player than me? I don't think so.

I kept stepping up to the plate on an annual basis and no one was coming along and taking me the way they had taken Luther Blissett.

I was becoming increasingly bitter. With Morton, with football, with life.

I asked for my first transfer before Morton's first season in the Premier League in the summer of 1978. By the time I left five years later I was tired of listening to my own voice.

I had been at the manager's door so many times demanding a move I was boring myself, let alone him.

I was fed up hearing the excuses and the ifs and buts.

I was having problems in my personal life by now. I could blame that on a million things, but bitterness is an unattractive trait and I was overflowing with the stuff.

It was not purely a bitterness with the people at Morton. I was bitter with the game of football in general, with the way it worked. I was putting my case for a move as honestly as I could.

Everytime I went asking for a move I would concede, 'okay, I don't do that, I don't do this. I accept my failings; but how come other people score fewer goals and THEY get moves?'

Maybe I did have more to give and maybe a move to a big club was the only way I was going to produce it.

The rumours were rife that Brian Clough wanted me at Nottingham Forest in 1979. They were European champions that year. Clough had done great things with John Robertson, another heavy smoking attacker perceived to be on the lazy side. Yet Robbo scored the winner in the 1980 European Cup Final when they beat Hamburg – 12 months after setting up the winner for Trevor Francis in the previous final.

Maybe if Clough had got me at that time and had offered me the chance to work with better players in better situations then I would have behaved myself. Perhaps not, we will never know. I do not think any of Clough's players were choirboys – but he kept on top of them, they got away with nothing.

That strong level of discipline might have been what I needed. Moving to Nottingham, Derby, London – anywhere – might have changed things for me. With a move your life starts over again and you have to fit in.

But when I was at my peak I was never presented with that opportunity. The opportunities presented themselves to Morton, but they never funnelled through to me.

The other side to that coin is that I need not chide myself over wasting anyone's money. I was never that great tabloid beast, 'the £1 million flop'. I never cost anyone a vast fee or huge wages. In retrospect I would have settled for the chance to become that man. I might at least have earned a few bob.

When I finally did move, Motherwell were a full-time club, that was the primary reason I went there. I hoped and prayed that full-time training might change things for me. For long enough I had been throwing reds on the roulette table, now the chance had come to go back in the black.

I rolled up at Fir Park a mere 10 days before the season started. For my first full-time pre-season in seven years this was a less than perfect scenario.

I had the classic introduction to training Jock Wallace style when he took me to Gullane Sands in East Lothian. At Rangers in his first spell this former fighter with the military bearing had forced his players to run up Scotland's steepest sand dunes in pre-season. Pictures of vomiting players bent over double became commonplace in the papers.

Bizarrely, I enjoyed the experience. I did not feel terribly good afterwards, I will concede that. But it was always a PR exercise as much as a serious training stint. When I got there a battery of photographers were awaiting my arrival.

From Jock it was all; 'look who I've got here coming to Gullane with me, Scotland's laziest player.' The gimmick value was obvious. We only went the once and never returned. The snappers got their pictures.

I was well behind in the fitness stakes, but Jock worked me morning, noon and night to try and get me fit. This should have been my fresh start; I would have picked Motherwell before Celtic at the age of 15 if they had wanted me. There had been a time when I would have killed a man for the chance to grace the amber jersey of my father's favourite team.

But in the event I was not at the club long enough to rebuild my knee muscles, let alone my career.

Jock played me against Morton in a League Cup game on the last day of August as another of his back-page grabbing stunts. The programme that night apparently carried a picture of me looking deeply unhappy after my £27,000 move from Morton. From £1 million to £27,000 was one hell of an indication of how far I had fallen from grace at Cappielow. Yet, that night, I scored in a 3–0 win.

I had problems with my cartilages after that; possibly because I was being worked too hard. I was over-training.

And then I remember playing around eight games, including a return to Cappielow in November when we lost 4–2. If my fitness was returning then it was being honed most in the reserves, not in the first team.

I had an argument early on with Jock when I was overworking concerning my recuperation from the cartilage problems.

He was pushing to get me fit and he felt I was dragging my heels – deliberately. He was wrong and I told him so. And he allowed me my say; something I had always valued as a footballer.

So we had a degree of respect and I can say in all honesty that I liked Jock Wallace; he might have been the man I needed.

By November 1983, however – just four months after my long-awaited arrival – he was on his way back to Ibrox. Past differences had been buried and after a dreadful period under John Greig, Rangers were returning to an old head for his second spell.

This, for me, would be the beginning of the end. Of my time at Motherwell and of my playing career. I was as fit as I had been since joining Morton and ready to challenge for my place and doing what I did best; scoring goals.

Then came the new manager Bobby Watson. A man who ended one of his first training sessions at the club by asking me loudly; 'do you have a career outside the game?'

I asked; 'why is that, what do you mean?'

His response that day in Airdrie remains with me vividly.

'Because you won't play at this club for me. You are not the type of player I want here.'

Which is one hell of an opening gambit from a new manager to one of his charges.

He had told me frankly I was not his type of player. Which prompted me to tell him he was not exactly my type of fucking manager. The die had been cast in our relationship.

He was true to his word. I never played another game for Motherwell and he never spoke to me unless it was absolutely necessary.

Fir Park has never been the largest of football stadia, so avoiding each other was a precarious business. But somehow we managed it until the week before Christmas.

There was a party laid on for everyone at the club and the instruction was quite simple; be there or else.

Feeling less than an assimilated member of the playing staff, however, I decided against taking my two sons Mark and Stephen along to the festivities. And when Bobby Watson realised this he fined me £100 for my alleged lack of yuletide spirit.

I was earning around £200 a week at the time and that equated to half a week's wages. Not a fortune, perhaps, but a significant sum for a young family with no win bonuses coming in.

And all because the manager, dressed from head to toe as Santa Claus, had been denied the chance to take centre stage before the Ritchie kids. It was laughable.

He claimed he had told everybody to bring their children. Maybe he did. But I felt no part of the club any longer and if I was no part of it then I was in no mood to pull the wool over the eyes of my boys.

I paid the fine and he outlined his view that he was doing this for the good of club morale.

I was predictably forthright in my response. I did not give two figs for his precious morale because my morale and that of my family was not especially high at that point. I wished him a happy Christmas as I slammed the door behind me.

This man could tell me nothing about morale at Motherwell FC. I had paid my way to watch this guy play for the club as a boy and had supported them all my life.

It was the final straw. I had a year and a half remaining on the contract I had signed for big Jock yet left Motherwell in January 1984. To my mind Bobby Watson had arrived on a massive ego trip and I was not about to jump aboard.

Watson was never interested in anyone but himself I felt.

He was a very successful businessman outwith football in steel stock holdings and drove a nice big Jaguar.

Business was his living, football was his pastime; a way of massaging his considerable self-esteem.

He pulled the same routine as he did with me on goalkeeper Nicky Walker; with one key difference.

Big Nicky secured himself a move to Rangers in the slipstream of Jock Wallace.

Me? I was free transferred. Following big Jock to Rangers was never really an option for me, though god knows I asked Nicky a few times in jest if he could fix it. I was invited to take myself where the sun did not shine in response.

The whole experience at Motherwell was a terrible personal body blow. Here I was again, my fresh start in ruins. Morton suddenly felt like a comfortable blanket I could never again hope to pull over my head.

I travelled to Blackpool and played a game down there for a manager called Sam Ellis. It was effectively a trial and a look round the place. When I travelled back home things were drifting badly.

How can I put this? I could no longer care less whether I ever played another game of football in my life. It was no great surprise, therefore, when Blackpool looked elsewhere.

Soon after that I received a telephone call from Davie Sneddon, manager of Stranraer offering me a trial.

And the penny dropped. This was it, the game was up.

I was about to turn 28, the peak year for so many competitive footballers and my career was effectively over.

Five years earlier I had been the best player in the country and everybody knew my name. Now? They spat it rather than said it.

I still had a young family to keep and a mortgage to pay.

I drifted around scraping work where I could. No easy task as the ravages of Thatcher's Britain took effect on the heavy industries in and around my locality. Unemployment among adult males was 16 per cent – higher in some areas – and unemployment was topping three million; the highest figure since the great depression of the 1930s. I was doing anything I could get my hands dirty on.

I worked in pubs, building sites, roads, whatever. For the family it was a hand to mouth existence.

You would suppose this might have been a significant source of stress and concern; but it bothered me less than it should have.

There was no need to concern yourself with the mundanities of everyday life if you spent two or three days drunk as a lord. And, by God, I did. I was back in the old routine.

If I was hardly a model of fitness when I left Motherwell – I had hardly played after all – then the months at the end of season 1983–84 did me no favours whatsoever.

When the phone finally did ring offering me a gig it was a familiar voice on the other end of the line.

Benny Rooney and Mike Jackson had also secured their escape from Morton and had formed a managerial team at Albion Rovers in the old Second Division. Could I now go along and help them to make up the numbers in a game at Dunfermline?

My relationship with Benny had not ended well at Cappielow but I was merely helping out; I was doing precious little else anyway. I certainly had not been training. But with £40 up for grabs for a one-off game of football this was no time for fool's pride.

This would be my first game in well over five months and, somehow, I lasted an hour. Not without breathing heavily, however, the pain of my lay-off kicking in well before my removal from the fray. We drew the game 1–1 – the first point Albion Rovers had won away from home all season if memory serves.

The next week, there was another call from Benny. It was the last game of the season and, again, they were short of players. Would I travel up to Arbroath and help them out once more?

Albion Rovers certainly had not won an away game all season, but I scored twice in a 2–1 win and we ended the season on a high.

We boarded the bus with a crate of beer and I sat down with Benny to chat, as you do.

As the bus trundled back south via some bleak east coast outposts my old manager told me he and Mike had been offered jobs at Partick Thistle and were off at the end of the season.

I wished him the best of luck and shook his hand; and I meant it. Two weeks later the Albion Rovers chairman Tom Fagan, who lived close to me in Mount Vernon, called me up and asked me if I fancied becoming the new manager of Albion Rovers.

I had a job in London lined up, at the Barbican. But it had not come through yet.

Here was an offer, in the meantime, I simply could not refuse. Perhaps I should have.

Chapter Eleven

Management

TOM FAGAN was the man at Albion Rovers, the only man who mattered.

He owned the club, he owned the ground and he also had a nightclub in Coatbridge, which – as is my wont – I had managed to be thrown out of more than once.

So when he spoke to me about becoming his new manager I agreed to go round and have a word.

People regard Albion Rovers in an unflattering light these days. How were they then? Even worse than they are now.

The club had won a League title in 1933–34 – a fact, which surprises a lot of folk – and had come second another three times. They had won a Scottish Cup at the end of World War One and a few Lanarkshire Cups along the way. Their record crowd was 27,381 for a game against Rangers in 1936. But this was 1984 and the average crowd by then was below 2,000. The glory days had long since gone never to be seen again.

Still, for me it was a start. It was an opening. The job I thought I had fixed up in London had not quite materialised yet. What had I to lose?

The most decent thing about the whole enterprise was the opportunity to meet the late, great Joe Baker.

Joe died back in 2003 and was a pretty unique man in the sense that he was born in Liverpool to Scottish parents and became an English international without having played in the English League. Owen Hargreaves is the only other player to have done it unless I am mistaken.

Joe moved north and grew up in Motherwell and actually played for Hibernian when he made his England debut in 1959 at the age of 19.

He was a fantastic guy who went on to play with Denis Law at Torino before finally playing in England for Billy Wright's Arsenal, Nottingham Forest and Sunderland. And despite that illustrious background he was destined to become my assistant manager.

He lived in Wishaw at the time and had been acting as the kit man, laying out strips and helping around the place. I had watched him picking up wet kits when I played there for a few games and thought it was ridiculous that a man with his background and experience should be wasted like that.

He had managed the club in season 1981–82 and had come back just to be around a dressing room.

I would listen to his stories and admire the guy. And if I was going to be the player-manager I wanted a man like that in the dug out as my eyes and ears.

I always remember the moment I told him that. I honestly thought the guy was about the cry with gratitude. He had been trying to escape the drink for a long time and had gone back scaffolding to earn a living. He was a top, top, humble man and a fantastic player in his day. Now here he was pitifully happy to be assistant manager at Albion Rovers. It was heartbreaking.

I was a manager at the age of 27. And what a way to start. We only had around eight players when I took the job in pre-season and the goalie John Balavage, who had come through the club's ranks, wanted a move away. He was a good keeper, but his mind was elsewhere.

My first task was to go through the list of free players. My second was to wrestle for an office.

The old groundsman showed me up to an old wooden office at the top of the stand.

The place was filthy and stinking. The paint was peeling and there was muck and dirt clotted to the walls and surfaces. It was a repulsive excuse for an office better suited to a Hobo. And I was not quite there yet.

An ashtray sat on the scratched and bare desk in the office. I am a smoker and like a fag, but this was ridiculous.

There must have been 100 cigarette ends in there and the place smelled of stale nicotine.

I looked around me and, not for the first time in my career, I thought to myself, 'what the fuck have I done?'

I had no sooner sat down at the rickety, shaky chair behind the desk when the door burst open.

A guy walked in, walked round the desk and without even acknowledging me, opened a drawer and started rummaging.

I said to him, 'what the fuck are you up to mate?'

He replied quite matter of fact, 'I'm checking the drawer. Looking for something.'

'I can see that,' I says. 'But this is my office.'

At which point he looks me up and down as if he thinks I am bull-shitting him and asks me straight, 'Oh aye, who are you?'

'I'm the manager of Albion Rovers,' I reply, chesting puffing outwards like a strutting pidgeon.

'Well, so far as I am concerned you're in MY fucking office,' he says. He went on to explain that he was the handicapper at the greyhound track, which lapped the playing surface at Cliftonhill Stadium, where they played.

'We share an office,' he explained. 'And I've been the handicapper here for 21 years.'

I had no answer to that. Albion Rovers managers were lucky to last 21 minutes never mind 21 years. He was right and so was I. Not only did I have a contender for a television documentary on 'Britain's Worst Offices', but I was sharing it.

When my new buddy left I looked at the sheet of paper containing my list of eight players and pondered what the hell to do next.

There was another page of free transfers in my back pocket, which the Scottish League had sent through. One name jumped out at me.

Bernie Slaven had played a couple of games for Queen of the South after leaving Morton and I knew, because he had spent some time at Cappielow with me, that he lived up in Castlemilk, one of Glasgow's more salubrious 'schemes' as they were called.

It was what Billy Connolly would call a 'desert wi windaes' and in one of my better moves I jumped in my car and made for Glasgow's south side immediately.

I knew where he stayed because I would drop him off from time to time and his dad was out in the garden.

'I'm looking for Bernard,' I announced.

'He's not in,' says his dad. 'He's doing some gardening work. Can I help?'

Frankly I doubted it, but I told him what it was about and he informed me Bernie was sitting on an offer from Shettleston Juniors.

I asked what he's been offered and the old man told me they were willing to stump up £250 for his services.

Bernie wanted a holiday before the season started and £250 would have let him do that with a bit of spending cash to spare in those days.

I was a bit downhearted by the news, but I was not beaten yet.

I went back to Coatbridge and sought out the chairman.

'I want £250 to pay for Bernie Slaven,' I announced with the minimum of fuss.

'Bernie Slaven?' asks old Tom Fagan. 'He's fucking hopeless. I wouldn't give you 250 pence for him. He was freed for a reason.'

I had a choice to make at this point. I either backed down and scored another name from the folded list in my back pocket or I made a stand. It was one of my easier decisions.

'I'm the fucking manager,' says I. 'And I need that £250 because we need to have 14 registered players before the first game of the season for the Lanarkshire Cup tie against Motherwell.'

'No. no. No can do,' he says.

'Well I'll tell you what then chairman. If this is the way it's going to be I won't be hanging out here long.'

It was a line every Albion Rovers manager since Archie Montgomerie in 1920 had probably used. And Tom Fagan had appointed most of them. He had heard it all before and he was unmoved.

'Suit yourself, you're not getting the money.'

I was trying to think my way around this and remembered the financial pay-off I had received to quit Motherwell.

I had a year and a half or two years of my contract to run and they paid me to leave. I was not desperate to spend it like this, but I did not see any other way out of it.

So I said to the chairman, 'I'll tell you what, I'll pay the £250 and I'll hold onto his registration because he'll score 100 goals here and I'll get the money for him when he does.'

The old boy was still unmoved. 'You do whatever you want. I'm not paying.'

So, just as I told his dad I would I went back to Castlemilk the following day and Bernie was there waiting for me. He was a nice lad, a non-drinker and a good character.

I told him I would match the £250 he had been offered by Shettleston and that we would pay him £12 a week.

Bernie did not fancy it. He had pals at Shettleston and he had all but made up his mind that was the plan.

But I was not having it. I convinced him to have one last try at the senior game, to avoid the kind of mistakes I had made and to make the right decision. Thankfully he bought it.

I told him I had faith in him. That I knew he could score goals. I wore the guy down and after two or three days convinced him to go for it.

He came and signed for Albion Rovers and the day I brought him in to sign old Tom came in the office and threw £250 down on the desk in old worn out, torn tenners and pound notes. It looked as if he had found the lot down the back of his living room couch 10 minutes earlier. There is every chance he had.

'Here,' he said with a stutter. 'If you want to do this do it. B.b.b.but don't come running to me when it comes b.b.b.back and b.b.b.bites you on the arse.'

It was not exactly a 'welcome to Albion Rovers Bernie, it's a pleasure to have you here'.

But I had got the man I wanted and got to keep my own £250 stuffed in my own pocket. Which, to my eyes, was where it belonged.

I thought I had won my first significant battle and had the old chairman where I wanted him; on the back foot.

No prizes for guessing who called it right, for once. Bernie Slaven scored 31 goals that season and ended the season as Scotland's top scorer. He fell out with Albion Rovers and ended up writing to every club in Scotland and England asking for a game. When Middlesbrough gave him a successful trial he left and Old Tommy Fagan pocketed £25,000. He played 381 times

I was sent out by Celtic to junior side Kirkintilloch by Rob Roy to toughen me up in 1972–73. It must have worked, I scored 33 goals in 21 games.

Here's me with my grandfather Andrew Gallacher. My old Granda had never seen a football game in his life until he went to see me play for Celtic Boys' Club.

Here's me with the family welcoming my Aunt Lizzie home from Canada.

On a family holiday 'doon the water' at Rothesay.

Proud as punch with my sponsored Ford Cortina supplied to me by Alexander's, the Ford dealership in Greenock.

Me, aged 12, on the putting green at Rothesay.

Belvidere Primary School Football Team, I'm the centre-half and captain. Top left, the assistant headmaster was Craig Brown, a future Scotland and Aberdeen manager. Miss Brown and Miss Craig (end) are the other teachers.

Bellshill YMCA Under-16 team. Top row second left, Harry Watson played for Crystal Palace. Striker Lee Miller's dad is third from right on the top row. Most of the team went on to play professionally.

Celtic Boys' Club before a foreign tour of Iceland in 1972.

Me in my Morton heyday; in action against Hibernian.

This is me flummoxing former Celtic full-back Andy Lynch. Happy days.

I always rose to the challenge of facing Sir Alex Ferguson's great Aberdeen side of the time. Here I am turning John McMaster inside out.

After leaving Morton I would finally join my boyhood heroes Motherwell. Here I am playing against them.

In Morton's yellow away shirt. Adidas Tango at my feet.

A celebration which suggested goalscoring was the easiest thing in the world. For a time it was.

Accepting the applause after scoring against Hibs at Easter Road. Arthur Duncan looks none too impressed. c.Greenock Telegraph

Again against Celtic, this time at Parkhead – although Morton wore the home kits. Tom McAdam is trying to work me out here.

Slotting home against my old team Celtic at Cappielow. Celtic 'keeper Pat Bonner is beaten with George McCluskey looking on.

With my back doing some defensive work here against the great Aberdeen team assembled by Sir Alex Ferguson. Willie Miller and Neale Cooper look on.

I'm not sure a large bottle of the sponsor's whisky was ever the best thing to be giving me for Man of the Match performances.

Scoring a couple of spot-kicks, the second against Rangers 'keeper Peter McCloy at Cappielow, with Ibrox players Colin Jackson, Jim Bett and Sandy Jardine hoping I miss...

Slotting a penalty against Airdrie at Cappielow. c.Greenock Telegraph

Andy is about to be tackled by Celtic's full-back Andy Lynch, 20 October 1979.

Young, carefree and skinnier than a butcher's dog.

for Boro and scored 147 goals, winning seven caps for the Republic of Ireland. I rest my case.

I signed another couple of guys at the same time as Bernie and – somehow – managed to put a team together. Cobbled more like.

I played a few games as well. We went to the old Muirton Park in the League Cup and we beat St Johnstone.

They were a First Division club at the time and we were in the Second Division.

All the while I was returning home after every training session to check the post. Managing Albion Rovers was fine but I had my eye on a new life and the job in London finally came through.

I had a start date close to Christmas, so I opted to carry on at Albion Rovers. We were mid-table, winning a few games, still in the League Cup, and I was enjoying it.

All except for one aspect of the job. The old chairman was keen on coming into the dressing room at half-time to voice his opinion on how the team were performing and to offer some tactical insight.

Now I tend to subscribe to the view that what the average football director knows about football equates to the centre of a doughnut.

But the old man had seen them all in and had seen a few out and it was his club. I indulged him.

One day he came in and went round the players imparting his pearls of wisdom.

We had a player called Vic Kasule, a Glaswegian winger of Ugandan descent who had been there a while by the time I arrived.

He told him and some of the other players they would not be getting their bonuses unless they bucked up their ideas.

When he was finished I escorted him to the door and opened it for his benefit. I thanked him profusely for his wise words.

'Thanks very much for that Mister Fagan, can't thank you enough.'

The first thing I did, of course, was to lock it to make sure he could not come back.

'Now listen to me lads,' I said. 'We listened to the old boy, we gave him five minutes of our time. Now we forget every word of his shite and we start to talk football again.'

Sure enough the boys went back out and won the game. Just as I had told them to do.

But not before a player called Tony Gallacher had hurt himself. Now this was a problem at Albion Rovers because we could not afford the services of a physiotherapist or a doctor.

There were 10 minutes to go and he looked as if someone has slashed him with a flick knife. His head was split open.

God rest his soul, on comes Joe Baker, assistant manager, kit man and all round legend, with a sponge and a bucket.

I ran over to him, took one look and saw he was finished.

I said to Joe, 'just get him in a taxi or even an ambulance and get him to Monklands Infirmary to get that treated. It's a bad one.'

What I did not see out the corner of my eye was the sight of the chairman slinking into the dug-out. Because Joe was on the pitch with a sponge he was not manning the technical area. No one was. Except for the chairman who was now ordering a substitute to warm up and get ready to go on.

I could hardly believe my eyes. My chairman was making decisions about substitutes without consulting his own manager.

I walked over to see what he thought he was playing at.

I knew Tony was finished, I knew we needed a sub on the pitch. Even as he was carted past me for the hospital though I was damned if I was letting the old man make the decision for me.

He was shouting at me to get someone on and I was shouting back along the lines of 'will I fuck'.

'I'm the manager,' I shouted. 'You're the chairman, get back up the stairs where you belong.'

So there we were arguing the toss for the whole crowd to see. There were not too many in but there were enough to see what was already blatantly apparent to me. My time was up.

'We've not got Gallacher at centre-half,' said the old boy. 'Put Green on at right wing and move someone else in there.'

Now I do not remember much about the player in question. He had not played much for me. What I did know was that he was a friend of the Fagan family.

So there we were having a huge row on the touchline and at the end of the game I knew what was coming.

We got back in the dressing room and he came in again, as if nothing had happened. Just as he had at half-time he started addressing the players and telling them all where they had gone wrong.

I'd already told the players that would not be happening again. Not on my watch. He had had his five minutes at half-time.

I could have fought him again, but instead I just sat down and had a long look around me.

And as I stared up at the cracks in the ceiling and the peeling paint it all became clear to me.

'What the bloody hell am I doing here?' I asked myself. I was 27 years of age, I had a job lined up in London. I did not want or need this shit.

I had never seen Hal Stewart behave like that at Morton. They say Bob Kelly, my old Celtic chairman, liked to pick the team in the old days. But that had quickly stopped when Jock Stein – a former Albion Rovers defender – had arrived. And if I wanted any respect here I would have to put my foot down. But I could not. Because I no longer cared if I had the job or not.

It was becoming not unlike a Brian Rix west end farce. He must have caught sight of my face when I was staring at the ceiling because after he left one of the other directors came down as I was changing.

'Andy, the chairman wants to see you upstairs in the boardroom.'

I agreed to go up before I left and as the players streamed out, their hair still dripping, they all waved farewell.

'Tuesday night training gaffer?'

'Aye, Tuesday night training lads.'

But as I sat there with a towel draped round me I knew there would be no Tuesday night training for me. There might be for them, but I would not be taking it.

I went to go in the bath and it was like staring into sheep dip. It was black and filthy and I went for a shower instead.

I came out, changed slowly and said cheerio to Joe Baker.

'See you Tuesday Andy?'

'Aye, see you Tuesday Joe.'

Joe still had the buzz. He still wanted to be in and around a football dressing room and was revelling in being off the booze. I do not claim to have known him well, but I liked him and I had a pang of regret about leaving him.

But I closed the door behind me and climbed the stairs to the boardroom.

I had barely entered the room when the old chairman started going on about my attitude and arrogance. I had heard this a thousand times before in my career, but I had no reason to take it from this guy. Not there, not then. Not in front of the other directors and lap dogs.

So it descends into another argument in the boardroom along predictable lines.

'I'm the manager,' I said. 'You have to let me manage.'

'Let you manage? Why should I when this is my club and I've always done it this way?'

We were going round in ever decreasing circles. Destined to meet with a crash in the middle.

'To be honest with you Mister Chairman, I've had enough. It's only been a few months, but I've had it.'

'Oh, you can't go. We've signed you for a year. You're under contract.'

'Naw,' I replied, expecting him to say that. 'You might think that Mister Chairman. But what I've actually been doing was putting myself through on 28-day contracts.'

'You what?'

'Aye, I'm the manager and I do the contracts. I've been taking my own contracts up to the SFA at Park Gardens every month. So my contract's up next week. Keep the week's wages and we'll call it quits.'

'You're going nowhere,' he roared, 'We've got you under contract.'

He was not quite grasping what I had said. I did not see the point in explaining it again.

'Listen, go and check the contract in that shit heap of a manager's office. It's in the handicapper's drawer.'

In one respect he was right. They could hold my registration and refuse to release it. They could prevent me from ever kicking a football again.

But by then that suited me just fine.

I turned to leave and took the stairs two at a time. At the bottom I walked outside and the first thing I saw was an enormous big metal bin where they put all the dog shit at the end of greyhound meetings three nights a week.

I opened the lid, took my boots out my bag and dropped them in among the stench and the shit.

I was finished with playing football. And with management.

I walked to my car and turned for one last look at the place. No disrespect to Albion Rovers, but I was finished with football to all intents and purposes.

Maybe if I had been 37 when I started managing instead of 27 my life would have been easier to handle. Maybe I would have been better able to handle the Tom Fagans of this world.

It was all just too soon for me. A bit too much too young.

When I look back now I recall the day I woke in London, some months later, and had the panic attack. The day I realised the game was up and I was finished. I knew I would never play again.

You could argue that I am one of the few unsacked football managers still here to tell the tale. I do not doubt they would have sacked me, but I walked on my terms because I had sorted out my own contract behind the old boy's back.

He thought at the time I must have an offer to go and play somewhere else.

But, to be honest, there was nothing in my performances at Albion Rovers to merit another club taking an interest.

I wanted to go down south and I would have done that Tom Fagan or no Tom Fagan. But the moment I lifted the lid of the shit bin, the game was up. It was the end of the road.

I coached again, when I came back up from London at the age of 33 or 34.

I worked under a fellow called Jimmy Dempsey, who asked me to take the reserve team and youngsters. And I got the bug again.

I helped Jimmy to bring George McCluskey, the former Celtic striker, to the club from Hibs. We had dropped down from the Premier League but we had a lot of good young boys like Paul McDonald coming through.

People kept thinking I would end up the manager at Morton. And, maybe inevitably, they did offer me a job at Cappielow after I had been at Accies a while.

They wanted me to come down and do some coaching of the kids and some commercial work. But there was a problem; they had forgotten to tell the manager Allan McGraw what they were planning.

It was a horrible mess. Hamilton had played Morton and after the game I bumped into the Morton director John Wilson, who owned the club at that time.

He spoke to me about coming down to Cappielow and I had a think about it and said yes.

I travelled down and spoke to another director Douglas Rae – now the owner and club benefactor – and he assured me it would be a mix of the commercial and coaching work and that it would all work just fine.

There was another fellow at the interview, the head of recruitment at a whisky company and I did not understand that. I still don't.

But either way we had a very productive meeting and they told me I would do a bit of coaching in the mornings of the reserves and with the first team under Allan and his assistant John McMaster.

I would then do the commercial work in the afternoon and I signed the contract.

Morton were playing that night and they drove me to the stadium that night and escorted me into the boardroom.

But there was just one problem. The team manager was there and he knew absolutely nothing about it.

Regrettably no one had told me whether he knew or not. In retrospect I should have asked a few more questions and found out about that. I was to blame both for that and for not listening to what was being said carefully enough.

But either way Allan blew his top. He said that if he had wanted to take a coach on he would have taken Jackie McNamara, my old pal.

He did not want me in or around the club. I was a threat to his job if things were not going well and all this came out in the boardroom.

It was an embarrassing scene, a hellish scene. I had not spoken to Allan in advance and, with the benefit of hindsight, I should have done. But I did not see the need at the time. I wish I had.

I hung around for a few months back at my old club. John Wilson paid my salary and I would go in every morning and sit in Allan's office where we would have a cup of tea and a blether.

There was no reason why we could not rub along and make the best of a bad situation. It was not one of our making particularly.

I respected the fact that Allan, a true Morton legend, said what he thought. He did not sneak around behind my back laying traps for me or undermining me.

I admired him for that and I was grateful. The problem was that I had left a full-time job at Hamilton Accies to move back to Greenock. So I had to hang around until something else came up – but I must have been in the job for less than five months in the end. It was an awkward scenario.

I spoke to Allan about it all after the event. But I was guilty of assuming things, which I should not have. You know what they say about the word 'assume'. It makes as 'ass' out of 'u' and 'me'.

It would only have taken five minutes of conversation with Allan to make it all perfectly clear. But I did not do it; I did not perform the due diligence. So I had no one else to blame but myself.

John Wilson told me to stay and see out my contract. But I was being embarrassed by myself, so god knows how other people saw me.

They gave me a car but there was no real job there. It was embarrassing for Morton and it was embarrassing for me and I had too much respect for both parties to let it carry on.

Eventually I went in one day and handed the keys to the car over. I was done.

I got a job selling hygiene and janitorial equipment. It was hard to leave Morton a second time, but it should have been clear to me from the start.

The only conceivable job I could do at Morton at that time was as manager. I was still a young man at the time and whatever I did I would always be a threat to the man in the hot seat if results went wrong.

Not because I was some kind of super manager, but simply because of my profile and reputation down there.

I have had various pals who have managed Morton and it is not bumping my own gums when I say there might have been times when I expected the phone to ring. That maybe I could help in some way.

But you think about it logically and it all becomes clear. Maybe they thought precisely the same thing as Allan McGraw.

Had that happened then it would never have been a case of me creeping around behind their backs.

That has never been my mode of operation and never would be. Right back to the days when Atholl Henderson took my reserve team peg at Celtic Park and I should have said, 'hold on a fucking minute here,' I have been an open book.

I do not work to an agenda. It might have helped me a few times if I had done.

But I never saw the point of making life difficult for other people and I always felt they would feel the same about me.

I was a success at Morton and I was an arsehole. But not in a backstabbing kind of way. I can honestly say that whatever bad things I have done in my life, they have not been pre-conceived.

I do not sit and think to myself, 'how do I work an angle for myself here?'

The mistakes I have made in my life have never been pre-conceived. And plentiful. Always plentiful.

Chapter Twelve

Back to Celtic

FOR ALL the success, which came my way at Morton, I never lost the feeling that leaving Celtic had been a huge mistake.

I turned my back on the greatest manager in the club's history to take my chances elsewhere. And you only get one chance at Celtic, they say.

So when Tommy Burns finally offered me the chance to go back to Paradise I was never likely to say no. Even if the job came complete with a blood-tipped knife.

On taking over as manager in 1994 Thomas needed someone to break up the club's long-running Celtic Boys' Club, a feeder club for the first team. I had done the coaching at Hamilton Accies for a time before the aborted Morton episode and then moving on to work with Jimmy Bone at St Mirren, taking the young players at the time. It was going well; I had young players in the first team at 16.

Kids like Ricky Gillies and Brian Hetherston had come through the Under-16s and reserves and I like to think I played a part in that. Joe Hughes, a talented and valuable scout for St Mirren over a number of years, found them and I got them in the team. They were dubbed, 'Andy's weans' by supporters and I admit I was tickled by that.

Campbell Money and Kenny McDowell, later to become a coach at Celtic and Rangers, were also there. We all worked hard and we got the best out of the meagre resources at our disposal.

When Tommy Burns and Billy Stark were at Kilmarnock, prior to being lured to Celtic in controversial circumstances by Fergus McCann, they came to play us one day. And the boys did us proud.

So when Tommy needed someone he knew and trusted to come and tackle the mounting problems in the youth ranks he turned to me.

He needed someone who knew the background. At the time a storm was about to break concerning serious sexual abuse of young players. The club were becoming aware of certain allegations and they wanted to cut the apron strings.

My name was suggested to Tommy as the man to turn the Boys' Club out, start our own Under-16 team and look after it.

The idea, not to put too fine a point on it, was to remove what Thomas described as a 'web of evil' at Celtic Boys' Club. Jim Torbett, coach of the Boys' Club and the owner of the Trophy Centre, would be convicted in 1998 of molesting former players, including Scotland international Alan Brazil, over a seven-year period. He was jailed for two and a half years. Another of the accused, Frank Cairney – a close ally of Tommy and my former Boys' Club mentor – was also accused concerning incidents preceding his resignation from the club in 1991, but acquitted due to insufficient evidence. Ironically, it was Cairney – my ex-wife's uncle – who suggested me to Tommy as a youth coach at a brain storming session in his front room. That I was being brought in then to break up the club he spent years nurturing was both awkward and ironic.

There were always rumours regarding despicable activities at the Boys' Club, but the harsh fact is this; until these matters arrive at your own door, until you experience the sheer horror of abuse in some shape or form, you can barely conceive of how it feels to be a victim or the parent of a victim.

I had only sampled anything of this nature on odd occasions as a young footballer when I had received a run home from training with some teammates from one particular coach.

We would desperately try to avoid being the last out of the car. Whoever left last risked feeling a clawing, clammy hand on the inside of their thigh in the car as they went to leave.

That happened to me once or twice together with what would become familiar advice.

'Don't you be wanking before the game this weekend,' would be the crude, bizarre jist of it.

I remember thinking that was strange at the time. Uncomfortable indeed. But for some reason it did not seem unduly strange.

I was a naive big boy. These days that would be regarded as sexual abuse, in those days people were ignorant of these things.

I was physically strong, but mentally weak. You hear about things like that but the reality seems surreal, the kind of thing that happens to the kids Esther Rantzen takes under her wing. Not in the real world, not in the West of Scotland.

Nevertheless, there were persistent rumours of wrongdoing at Celtic Boys' Club and something had to be done.

Tommy asked me to come back to Celtic on a part-time basis at a charity event in Clydebank one Saturday morning. I would be in charge of running the show at Under-16 level – a stage Tommy regarded as very important to the development of players.

He offered me £100 a week to do the job. Initially Celtic only wanted to pay me £65 a week to work with David Hay, the chief scout brought in to offer an experienced hand at Tommy's side. A grudging approach to paying a fair day's pay for a fair day's work would become a feature of my return to the club.

My move was rubber-stamped and I was appointed to my special mission. When they discovered precisely what my role would be, it did not please the hierarchy of the Boys' Club, who had built up an empire around themselves. They held significant sway at Celtic Park and now I was threatening this.

Very quickly after that the game was up for them anyway. *The Daily Record* newspaper published a series of highly damaging allegations, which ended in witnesses coming forward by the dozen. A high profile and extremely embarrassing court case ensued in Glasgow and that allowed me to get on with familiarising myself with the set-up at Celtic Park.

I was working by day with a chemical firm at the time and I had the time to go in and sit chatting with Tommy in the sauna on a Friday morning. We also spoke on the phone every second night when he would check I was settling in. My role was about to change for the better, however, in the most innocuous of circumstances.

Tommy asked me and Tom McAdam, a distinguished defender with the club in the 80s and a coach at the club, to take the Under-18s to New York for a tournament. I had made all the arrangements with work and was due to fly to New York on the Tuesday morning when I went shopping for a new door for the house before my departure. I was sliding the door from its stand in the DIY store when I popped a disc in my back. I was in agony. And it got worse when another disc popped out in sympathy seconds later.

I was prostrate. I made it home and lay on the carpet until a doctor arrived. I was admitted to hospital immediately and spent five and a half weeks in Monklands Infirmary with a serious back complaint.

I missed the American trip and took sick leave from my day job. Work was impossible, let alone training young kids.

Eventually I was discharged from hospital on a dreadful day for Celtic – one of the blackest days in the short life of Thomas Burns. And in Celtic's recent history.

Tommy had led the club back to the League Cup Final where they were to play First Division Raith Rovers at Ibrox. A five-year trophy drought seemed certain to end. Or so we all believed.

I returned from sick leave to attend the game and when they arrived back at Parkhead after a penalty shoot-out defeat to the Fifers I was the only person in the players' lounge who looked – if not felt – worse than Tommy Burns.

Charlie Nicholas, in his second spell at the club, had scored six minutes from the end to put us 2–1 ahead. The Cup was coming home.

But then Gordon Dalziel, who would go on to manage Rovers, swooped to head the ball into the net at the death to take the game to extra-time.

When it went to penalties poor Paul McStay, the captain, stepped up to see his effort saved and Raith won 6–5 in the shoot-out. For everyone at Celtic the numbness struggled to overcome the anguish.

I was on a mass of painkillers and Tommy could have used half a dozen of what I was on that night as well. To say my old friend was completely and utterly devastated would be an understatement. I swear that I witnessed Thomas age 10 years that night. He was beginning to go grey on his arrival at Celtic to a slight degree. That game exacerbated his descent from burning red hair to being white-headed in a relatively short space of time.

I remember we got off the bus from Ibrox after the longest journey ever and I made for the gent's toilet just inside the glass-fronted Celtic reception area. Thomas followed me in.

We stood side by side at the urinals and the conversation went something like this.

'You alright?' I asked, in what must rank as the stupidest question ever addressed to another human being.

'I just want to go home and sit in the big chair,' mumbled Tommy in response, staring straight ahead as he said it.

The big chair, to the uninitiated, was Tommy's place of respite in his front room. In times of self-doubt, anger or crisis Tommy would sit there late into the night, thinking, pondering, contemplating.

'Where do I go from here?' he asked as much to himself as to me.

'You go to Easter Road on Wednesday night and you get on with beating Hibs, my friend,' I said. It was the best I could muster and it was an exercise in futility.

To Thomas the thought of another game of football at that point was as painful as my shattered back. 'There's nothing else for it Tommy. The days of dancing round the park like Nobby Stiles are over. These are the bad days, accept it and get through it.'

With that we meandered through to the player's lounge where there was nothing awaiting us. Not so much as a cup of tea, let alone celebratory champagne.

We ordered some food up for the players who had come back with us and some of the wives. It's no exaggeration to say it was like attending a wake. People were incapable of sustaining eye contact. I remember sitting with Tosh McKinlay, who had only recently arrived as a left-back at the club and telling him that he had to lift himself as well. We all did. Yet to most people that game was unthinkable.

Rosemary would later tell me that Thomas did indeed head for the Big Chair that night. He sat until the early hours of the morning thinking, just thinking. And when he stood up and got some sleep he took his players to Edinburgh on the Wednesday and drew 1–1 thanks to a John Collins goal. Life had to go on, however unsatisfactorily, Celtic ending the season a distant fourth in the League.

For me life was being made a misery by the discs in my back. Even standing upright was an effort. I was in a lot of discomfort. It did not help that I had fallen out with another of the youth coaches, Willie McStay.

Willie was co-ordinating the youth set-up and the Under-18s and we had a confrontation over who picked the Under-16s and various other issues – to me it was my team. So we had quite a row one day and we needed some clarification from the team manager. To me a manager is no such thing unless he controls team selection.

Maybe we should have sorted it out man to man, but I knocked on Tommy's door and asked him to clarify the matter.

Willie and I were summoned in and sat down on the other side of the desk where Tommy passed judgment; making it clear that I picked the Under-16 team and not Willie.

McStay was unhappy I had gone straight to Tommy over his head – and looking back he had a point actually. But as we were leaving the office Tommy pursued me and stopped me in the corridor.

'You're not enjoying this Trumpton are you? You've lost the sparkle for this job.'

If the truth be told the combination of my back and the politics involved in breaking up Celtic Boys' Club was draining me of my energies. The politics at Parkhead could sap a man's will to go on.

I said to Thomas straight: 'No, I'm not enjoying this and I'm glad you asked me.'

'Come in for a sauna on Thursday,' said Tommy.

When I turned up for that he ended our chat by giving me a video of NAC Breda in Holland. There was an American player we wanted to have a look at on there and he wanted me to undertake the task.

'I want you to go and do some scouting work for Davie Hay,' said Tommy. 'I want you to go and get yourself really involved. Davie does not fancy a lot of the travelling and stuff, he feels the job is not for him now. He wants a general manager's job or a shift upstairs.'

This was fine by me. I did not care where I was as long as I was some use to Tommy and Celtic. Davie certainly had no problem with me coming on board, the man was extremely helpful to me and for that I was grateful. Still am.

The task from then on was to help dig up the players we needed to halt the dominance of Rangers. Players who would have the fans off their seats and rejuvenated by the sight of a team in green and white playing football the Celtic Way. If those players came complete with character flaws and a bit of arrogance then so be it.

The era of the Three Amigos was about to commence.

Chapter Thirteen

The Three Amigos

*MY NEW role suited me just fine. I could disappear into a darkened room
with a video or three and watch football for hour upon hour. And I was being
paid for it.*

The level of desperation of agents to get their players into Celtic was an eye
opener. There were motorcycle couriers roaring up with special deliveries
from all over the world. The Milk Tray man had nothing on this.

Most were of little or no interest. But in there somewhere there had to be
the odd gem. It was my job to find them.

I went with the video of NAC Breda Tommy had been given by the chief
scout Davie Hay to a back room with a television off the tunnel. It was a
Friday and the videos started rolling in at a frightening rate. Most of them
would end up in a plastic supermarket bag in a cabinet.

But the most productive viewing still came from that first video produced
by Tommy in the sauna. There was a guy who played wide right for them by
the name of Ernie Stewart. We made a pot of tea, dug out the Jaffa Cakes
and invited Packie Bonner into join us. Tommy and Packie were chatting and
the phone was ringing off the hook and I am watching Ernie Stewart.

But every time he threw in the cross this giant of a striker was getting on
the end of it. Who the hell was this?

I got to imagining this 6ft 3in giant in a hoops jersey bullying Richard
Gough and the Rangers defence all over the place. We had Simon Donnelly,
Brian McLaughlin, Marc Anthony and a team of relative midgets up front
and here was this big guy running out of ways to score goals.

I drew Tommy's attention to the video Davie had sourced and then heard
nothing more of it until him and Billy Stark went on a foreign mission
around the time of Celtic's annual staff Christmas night in a horrible hotel
off Sauchiehall Street on a night to drown cats.

They arrived at the back of 10pm to announce they were signing a guy by
the name of Pierre van Hoojidonk for £1 million. Davie Hay had raved about
him. We had a new centre-forward.

The stories would grow over time of the disruptive and arrogant
Dutchman who turned down a £7,000 a week contract dismissively,
describing £360,000 a year as 'alright for the homeless' when he was offered
a new contract close to the end of his time at the club. By then there were
unsettling influences clinging to his coat-tails in Glasgow; the adoration and

attention had gone to his head. He was a young man and he changed. By the time he moved to Nottingham Forest he was in the big League. He had always had great aspirations and as a kid adopted at a young age perhaps that was understandable.

But that was a different Pierre from the one who had arrived at Celtic. From the outset he was a lovely boy. A big, quiet and soft fellow, polite to a fault. He appreciated the opportunity he had been given to come to a club like Celtic. He needed a step up and Celtic badly needed him to return the favour.

I consider myself privileged to have known Pierre at the time he joined the club. Thereafter he was never seen again.

At Forest he caused absolute mayhem under my chum Harry Bassett and followed that with more mayhem everywhere else as well. The only club who seemed capable of taming him – and he was older by that time – were Feyenoord, where he won a UEFA Cup medal. In Turkey it was the bad Pierre who came out to play.

If I am honest then I had to say I was not entirely surprised by what developed with Pierre or any of the talents who followed him into Celtic Park.

We were in a marketplace where we needed charisma. The club needed a lift, Tommy demanded it. He had a vision of passing football, which embraced temperamental genius, whatever the baggage attached.

We were desperate at the time to sign Georgi Kinkladze from Manchester City for £5.5 million. That was a king's ransom to Celtic. We needed to break the bank to excite the crowd and fill a spanking new 60,000 stadium. There was too much negativity around the place and the guys we needed were not to be found in the Scottish Premier League.

We knew Fergus McCann was reluctant to spend big. But we still needed players like Kinkladze from somewhere. Which meant we had to gamble on the slightly flawed maestros of this world. We were not shopping in Harrods, we were shopping in the Harrods Clearance Warehouse for the slightly frayed items others did not have to gamble on.

Tommy had heard that a guy Paolo Di Canio was available in the summer of 1996 and he asked me one day if I knew anything about him. He had become available and wondered what I thought.

I was honest. I did not know a great deal, but I knew a man who did. I phoned a guy Pierro Esposto who was very close to Juventus, Di Canio's club. I also knew him to be an excellent judge of a player. To me he was an Italian with a Scottish mentality. If anyone knew whether this guy was cut out for life in Glasgow this guy did.

His words to me were, and I quote: 'Paolo Di Canio is a major talent. And I mean a major talent. He will excite the fans and have them in raptures, standing on their seats. But he will make your manager an old man in 12 months. He will have everyone around the club in turmoil.'

To this day I have never heard a more accurate player assessment in all my many years in professional football.

I gave Tommy Esposto's number to call him. If he was worried about premature ageing then he did not show it. We paid a modest fee of £700,000 plus add-ons and whether you view that as a bargain depends on your value system.

In his season at Celtic this mad Italian bordered on being a genius at times. But we had been told he would cause havoc while drawing mass adulation from the fans. That was precisely the way it worked out.

Jorge Cadete was the third member of the unholy trinity. Had Fergus McCann had any hair left on his head this wee fellow would have put paid to that.

Tommy had seen Cadete rout Scotland in a 5–0 thrashing in Lisbon; 'the night a team died' as the former national coach Andy Roxburgh memorably put it. Cadete, it's fair to say, had dealt out the fatal blows. Not until Sir Bobby Robson brought Barcelona to play a friendly at Parkhead did we give serious thought to bringing him in however. Prosinecki and De La Pena dazzled folk before we retreated to the coaches' room afterwards for a chat with Sir Bobby – a man Fergus would later try to bring to Celtic as head coach. Unsuccessfully.

Bobby had Jorge under his wing during a successful spell at Sporting Lisbon and when we said we were looking for a striker to play last man on the shoulders of the defenders, Jorge's name came up. We learned he might be available and how much money it might take to sign him.

Typically for the period he had his problems. Like van Hooijdonk and Di Canio he had an erratic streak and arrived at a time when he might best be described as a sick pup. He had problems in his marriage, deep ranging personal problems and a cash flow problem. But what a player for £650,000. Sure it was a gamble, but gambles did not always go against you.

Signing players for that price was rather like the privatisation ads for national utility companies being sold off. 'Shares can go up or down' they always told you. Well, the same has always applied in the football transfer market.

You could argue that we won the bet when we went out the next season and spent £650,000 again on a certain Henrik Larsson esq.

And to this day I would argue that we lost anything when we brought in van Hooijdonk, Di Canio and Cadete. We needed a spark and in a season where we never lost a League game, yet still failed to win a title, they sure as hell gave us it. Had the late Jim Farry, the former SFA secretary who fell on his sword for failing to push Cadete's registration through on time, been brought to book earlier I still believe Rangers would never have made it to nine-in-a-row.

In the end a superb Ibrox team beat us to the punch once again and Tommy took that hard. Here was a man who took failure of any description hard.

Rangers had fine players at the time; they were paying what Fergus McCann used to call 'top dollar'. In contrast he was reluctant to pay a thin dime more than was required for anything.

Rangers had Gascoigne and Laudrup augmenting a solid spine. They had fantastic team spirit and even when they bought top players and looked to be unbeatable they kept building from a position of strength. Celtic have never done that in their history. Credit where credit is due must go to Walter Smith for his first spell in charge. They had the hex over Tommy and they were a hard, hard team to beat.

We were closing the gap. We were close where the gap had hitherto been enormous. But we were not winning the League – and to Thomas Burns that constituted failure. And from the first day I met that man to the last, failure was a concept, which sat poorly on his proud shoulders.

He had a beautiful family, his faith and a wonderful life outwith football. But Celtic were his passion. Winning was his reason for being; a view magnified a hundred fold by the fact he was a diehard supporter of the club. Celtic had to win and though he knew that the reasons for failure could not entirely be laid at his door – there were others in the boardroom and on the park who were also culpable – it did not make the pain any duller.

Fergus and Thomas had never had a great relationship anyway and every defeat towards the end exacerbated the level of tension. Every time Tommy went upstairs to speak to the Managing Director he would return downstairs in a worse mood than that he had gone with. It was best to avoid the nitty-gritty of what had happened in conversation – his anger on these occasions was palpable.

I had known Tommy Burns as boy, man, husband, father and grandfather and you would be hard pressed to draw a bad word about anyone from him for most of that period.

But towards the end of his time in charge he would be angry, bitter and frustrated. That never lasted particularly long. There was never abuse, never any bad language, that was not Thomas.

But he and Fergus were in a state of permanent conflict. He would appeal for money to do this or that – and the majority shareholder, the man who appointed him, always had other ideas.

It had gone wrong from the start; from the court case, which arose from his move to Celtic from Kilmarnock. The Ayrshire club argued that Fergus had illegally tapped Tommy against FIFA rules. McCann had given evidence in the dock and he did not lose too many court cases in his time – of which there were plenty.

But Tommy's evidence did not relate to what Fergus had testified. We did not know at that time that the truth according to Fergus McCann was different from the truth according to Tommy Burns. Perhaps the wisest move for Tommy might have been to adapt his version of events slightly in the cause of harmony and industrial relations. But that was not Thomas.

They had got off on the wrong foot as Kilmarnock won their case and it was all downhill from there. When Tommy signed a cheque for £2 million for Motherwell's Phil O'Donnell with Fergus out of the country it soured the milk that bit more.

I would not say it was personal. Not initially at least. It was more a battle of financial will – and there could be only one winner.

When we lost the Scottish Cup semi-final of 1997 to Falkirk it was a public humiliation for a man who didn't deserve it. Self-doubt crept in after that. You try to keep up the public persona of being completely on top of the job. But when Thomas was on his own, when he sat in the Big Chair in Newton Mearns, the doubts tortured a sharp footballing brain.

I used to think the players could never be as committed to Celtic as Tommy Burns was.

Deep down in his heart of hearts Tommy felt he was not ready to manage Celtic. But everybody he spoke to – myself included – said the same thing.

'Thomas,' I said, 'you might only get one opportunity to do this. You have to take the job.'

If he had knocked it back it might never have come around again. As it transpired he ended his life where he wanted to be – in the Celtic dugout as a coach under Gordon Strachan.

It was a rollercoaster ride, but Thomas Burns lived the Celtic dream. And that was all he ever wanted.

Chapter Fourteen

A Touch of Dutch

WITH HIS perm bursting out in a hundred directions and a stocky, squat frame Wim Jansen arrived at Celtic to something approaching ridicule.

Those who underestimated this quietly spoken man were entirely wrong. Behind the physical façade lay a steely and stubborn mindset in the finest Dutch tradition.

I was a bit perturbed by the fact people called Wim odd from the off. Perhaps he did not have the Jock Stein stature or presence. Jock was not a tall man, but he was heavy and he conveyed this vast physical presence when he entered a room. Equally Billy McNeill was the son of a sergeant major and walked with that same military bearing. Pidgeon chest out, head upright, you could imagine big Cesar with a stick under his arm at Parkhead. But Wim was not like that.

He was quiet and respectful and he listened politely to what you had to say. He was soft spoken – but anyone who looked beyond the physical characteristics could see that a steely little man hid behind the outward exterior.

From the very start Celtic and Wim Jansen was a marriage doomed to end in divorce. Background politics had pulled Tommy Burns down in the three years he spent at the managerial helm and they did not take too long to pull Wim Jansen down either.

The reasons for that were numerous and varied. It had plenty to do with Jock Brown, the general manager Wim had a venomous relationship with and much to do with Fergus McCann's combative running of the club. But it was not only that. Both Wim's backroom team and the players had a lot to say for themselves in that dressing room and the competing elements were what might be described as an unhealthy soup; a thoroughly bad mix.

It all got off to a bad start.

Jock Brown had appointed Eric Black, the former Aberdeen striker and current Sunderland assistant, to run the youth set-up along with Kenny McDowall, now assistant to Ally McCoist at Rangers. And Wim, denied a say in the process, did not want them. It would possibly be accurate to say that Murdo McLeod, appointed Wim's number two during the pre-season and a major ally of the Dutchman, did not much fancy them either.

It did not help that Jock Brown himself had been appointed at a time when David Hay, a hero in the eyes of the fans, wanted the General

Manager's job for himself. David also had a good mutual relationship with Wim, which resulted in the development of powerful alliances.

So it was never a happy ship from the off. They all went off to Holland for a bit of training and squad 'bonding' in July 1997. Thankfully I was not there, but I can well imagine that was the breeding ground for the viper's nest Celtic Park would become in the months which followed.

There were a lot of people jockeying for better positions within the football department and a lot of people unhappy with who was arriving at the club; Eric and Kenny for example had a very difficult time from the start I believe, with little in the way of conversation between them and Wim. It must have been hard for those guys.

In my position your first thought was always the same; what's going to happen to me here? Do not listen to what anyone else tells you. There is no one in football with an ounce of sense who does not worry when a new coach comes in. The concerns are always the same; am I going to be here this season doing a job or not?

The Dutch footballing community tend to think primarily about themselves and adopt an unsentimental approach to their decision-making. If you look at the history of the national team Euro 2008 may be the first time in living memory they avoided self-combustion on the big occasion. They do not hold back, these guys. So of course I worried for myself when Wim arrived.

Here was a man with no Celtic background. This was not my pal Tommy Burns any longer; he had no loyalty to me or anyone else. But he developed feelings for Celtic in a very, very short space of time. And he was fine with me if the truth be told.

He does not look much like a football manager they said. To which my response is always the same, 'what precisely does a football manager look like?' I suppose I have never been the type of person to worry too much about people's appearance.

When Wim arrived at Celtic as Tommy's replacement after a lengthy search, he had been one of the finest Dutch players of his generation; he had all the traits of every football man from that country I have ever met. Sadly I have never met Rinus Michels, the mastermind behind the great Netherlands teams Wim played in which routinely reached the latter stages of major international championships in the 1970s. But my old Morton teammate and football union man Tony Higgins has; and he says it's a joy to spend an hour in the man's company. In their ideology the Dutch are invariably way ahead of everyone else.

In the 1950s and 60s they used to laugh at Dutch football.

Then came Rinus, Johann Cruyff, Feyenoord's victory over Celtic in the 1970 European Cup Final, the great Ajax team, which took their crown and the oranje sides who stormed their way through World Cups playing Total Football. And what people had forgotten when Wim Jansen was introduced to the sound of tumble weed as the new head coach of Celtic was that he was part of all that. A major part. He had played for Feyenoord when they defeated Celtic in the 1970 European Cup Final and stayed at that major club for 15 years as a player. He had been the quiet man of the national team, which reached two World Cup Finals in 1974 and 1978. He was even one of the men Archie Gemmill danced round on the way to THAT goal in Argentina. And yet on rolling up at Celtic Park the headline in the country's biggest selling tabloid of the time described him as; 'The Second Worst Thing to Have Hit Hiroshima,' in response to his record in his previous job in Japanese football.

We should have expected it. Scottish football and its followers have never really come to terms with the use of the term 'technical ability'. It is an alien concept. In the West of Scotland technical ability was defined as the capacity to make a decent footstool at Motherwell College. So Wim's arrival complete with the perm, the slightly broken English and all the talk of Dutch thinking was received with something approaching bemused insularity. What they had all forgotten was that you do not play in two World Cup Finals if you are some kind of farmer's scarecrow.

I remember the night we played Liverpool in the UEFA Cup in October 1997. No one gave us a cat in hell's chance before we drew 2–2 with them in Glasgow, an amazing solo goal from Steve McManaman robbing us of a major scalp after recovering from the loss of an early goal.

The first leg at Parkhead was held up for a bit to allow the crowd in and I wandered down the tunnel for a few minutes to hear the Celtic and Liverpool supporters united in an emotional rendition of You'll Never Walk Alone.

I went back to the dressing room immediately and interrupted Wim to ask if he had a minute. Puzzled, he silently followed me back towards the pitch side as I nodded to the stands. He stood looking all around him at the sight and sounds I had confronted moments before. He did not say a word, he just stood there milking it all in; a momentous scene which encapsulated what Celtic are all about. And I thought to myself; 'he gets this, he's got the bug'.

Wim turned as quietly as he had come to return to the dressing room with a new determination to do the job he had taken on for these people, his new disciples.

I am not suggesting that he knew nothing about Celtic before his arrival. Feyenoord were also a big club in Holland and it did not take long for him to see that the fans were on the same wavelength or that their old De Kuip home shared characteristics with Celtic Park. Both sets of fans were a bit more working class in outlook, convinced that the 'other' team – be it

Rangers or Ajax – were the establishment team. But that night against Liverpool was the night the true size of the club dawned on Wim. He knew about their reputation abroad and Celtic were clever; they introduced their new coach to their worldwide fans quickly and he responded to that.

It was a pleasure to work with him and I actually respected him greatly. I enjoyed every conversation I had with the man, but I will be honest. I was also disappointed in him.

Not because he did anything out of the ordinary to me. I could not say here that he improved or detracted from my life in either way. I enjoyed all the football dealings I had with him despite the fact that I never knew him well enough to call him a friend as such. We did not socialise or eat out and knew little of each other's background, but that was fine.

What disappointed me was the fact that he allowed a poisonous situation to develop at Celtic without ever really trying to sort it out. And that he allowed people outwith the club to think he might stay when he knew very early indeed that he would leave at the end of the season.

He based too many of his opinions on people at Celtic Park on first impressions or what others were whispering in his ear; he made up his mind at an early stage and never truly veered from that thereafter. I sometimes wonder whether he would have done things any differently at Celtic Park given the chance to reserve judgment without being pushed in any one direction by his closest aides. Possibly not.

We had worked together on some signings and potential future signings. Not least Paul Lambert, brought back from Germany for £2.5 million before the turn of the year. But after Lambert, a former Motherwell midfielder, arrived from Borussia Dortmund as a European Cup winner in a significant signing coup Wim said something to me which rung the alarm bells in my head.

'There will be no more signings here,' said Wim. 'We will not sign another player, so go and have some fun.'

And he meant it. So much so that I took a week's holiday in Marbella in the full knowledge that I now had plenty of time on my hands for the rest of the season. The game, as they say, was well and truly up for Wim Jansen and Celtic.

The relationship had broken down already and I believe that a decision had already been made by Wim to leave Celtic. If not then he was 70 per cent of the way there. Win or lose the League, stop Rangers winning 10-in-a-row or not, it was never going to make any difference. Wim was for the off.

You could argue that it was to his credit that he kept it as private as he did. Not until he decided to break the news of a break clause in his contract on the club's official Celtic Hotline phone service did any of the players know what was afoot.

So his professionalism in the dressing room was beyond reproach. They never saw a chink of resentment or anger at the way his relationship with Jock and Fergus was deteriorating. And that was a team always on the lookout for the merest sniff of weakness. Guys like Craig Burley and Alan Stubbs could smell developments in the air. But they missed that one and that was to Wim's credit at a time when the team were going for the League.

Neither can you get away from the fact that here was the man who brought Henrik Larsson to Celtic for a bargain basement price of £650,000.

Wim's first act had been to wave farewell to Paolo Di Canio in a 'trade' for Regi Blinker with Sheffield Wednesday. The fans feared the erratic Italian might never be replaced – how wrong they were.

There are few who would dispute the fact that perhaps Henrik is the only one of the modern day players who could have muscled his way into the Lisbon Lions. The way he transformed a Champions League Final for Barcelona against Arsenal proved it. But life did not start so well for Henrik at Parkhead.

Things changed significantly for the better the day the former Scotland left-back Tosh McKinlay stuck the head on him at training at Barrowfield. I would imagine now that Tosh wishes he had not done something, which profoundly affected his own Celtic career. And it did absolutely nothing for Henrik's good looks either. But I always got the feeling that Henrik rolled up believing that he was better than everybody at Celtic Park. And he was beginning to portray that in a way unmistakable to the other players.

So in more ways than one Tosh stopped him in his tracks. And thereafter Henrik's attitude and professionalism improved quite radically. Suddenly here was a player thinking, 'yes I'm better than these players, but I will only show that on the park, not off it'.

From that point Henrik became a bit more aloof and sensitive to the whole situation. But his record thereafter showed this much; Tosh McKinlay did him the world of good.

If Henrik was the best of Wim's signings then others enjoyed variable levels of success. Jock Brown had wanted to sign Darren Jackson from Hibernian from the off – and Wim's view on the matter might have been evident in the fact that Darren's appearances were best described as sporadic. Wim did not rate him, simple as that.

Harald Brattbakk also arrived from Rosenborg, a bespectacled accountant who looked as if he should be auditing the local grocer's books rather than playing for Celtic. Davie Hay knew his agent from the time he had spent as a manager in Norway with Lillestrom.

Davie was under pressure to sign a striker, Harald had a good pedigree, Davie had seen him, knew he was available, knew how much he would cost and did his homework.

But it would be fair to say this. For all the garlands Harald attracted when he slotted home the goal against St Johnstone that won the League, he was a failure at Celtic Park. With a price tag of £3.5 million he could never thereafter be anything else.

Thereafter the football department were forced to change the way we went about signing players. For £3.5 million you expect a player to be successful. If he's not something has to change; you have to get value for money.

As a result the board insisted that a player had to be watched six times before he could be signed. The manager had to see him twice, David Hay had to see them, I had to see them, everyone had to see them. And yet in the aftermath of Wim's Paul Lambert bombshell there was precious little need for watching any players; Wim had no plans to sign another player for Celtic.

For years I was expected to attend a managerial meeting at Celtic Park on a Monday morning where I would explain where I had been that weekend, who I had watched and why. By the end of the season my reports were a work of fiction.

Wim had told me to tell 'them' – them being Fergus, the financial director Eric Riley and the senior management of the club – nothing. But I still had to keep up a facade of providing information otherwise I would have been out of a job.

Wim had told me before Lambert's arrival that he wanted me to go to Japan to sign Hidetoshi Nakata and Patrick Mboma. The coach had worked in the J-League and knew that Nakata was destined to become the first Japanese superstar in Europe years before Shunsuke Nakamura was ever heard of. The marketing potential for Celtic was obvious. Shirt sales, television revenue, the lot. Mboma, meanwhile, was a Cameroon international, a powerful dynamic striker.

But after Lambert came the end of the party was nigh and the instructions changed.

When I asked Wim if I should still be pursuing these guys the answer was to the point: 'No. Forget it.'

That was when I decided that a week in Marbella might be a good move. So did Wim, who would phone me when I was by the poolside with a smile in his voice in that unmistakable Dutch accent: 'How's the sunshine over there Andy? Are you enjoying your beers, yah?'

I could hardly tell him no. Or that I was actually becoming increasingly uneasy with the whole situation. Everyone who knew what was happening felt the same.

I wanted my job to continue and progress at Celtic Park. I wanted to help find the next big thing, the next Pierre van Hoojidonk or Larsson; that was my job. It was fine for Wim and the others to sacrifice jobs before moving onto their next £1 million contract. These guys could jump in the Clyde and come out with a salmon in their pocket.

But I had a mortgage and a family to support. And I was never on a million pound contract. Nothing like it.

When I came back from Spain it became a war of attrition with the club management. I would go to Ipswich to watch a young Kieron Dyer and come back to tell them I had been watching someone else entirely.

Jansen would say to me, 'tell these people what you know and they will know the same as you. And knowledge is everything.'

The reason was simple; he wanted to give Fergus, Jock and the rest the run-around. He had already made his decision and this was now effectively a work to rule.

All the while the tension behind the scenes and on the park was becoming unbearable. Wim was withdrawing from the club and the general manager Jock Brown was reacting by rowing with players and anyone else in his path.

His relationship with Lambert, a player who believed Jock had never wanted him in the first place, was poor.

Rumours were circulating that Jock was telling folk Lambert was not good enough to play for Celtic and Paul had heard them.

So I tried to calm troubled waters by putting the two of them together in Jock's office and saying, 'come on, sort this out'. The next thing I knew there was all sorts of commotion and I was in there separating the two of them. They were arguing ferociously and I virtually had to drag them apart before Lambert stormed away in disgust. Jock stood there demanding I get Paul back in the office so he could tell him how brainless he was being. Well, there is one thing Paul Lambert has never been – and that is stupid.

For the likes of me it was always a case of straddling the two camps, trying not to be dragged into the internecine warfare going on behind closed doors.

There was a perception on the part of some that I got on well with Jock, better certainly than the supporters who wanted his head on a silver platter. Many suspected this former journalist, lawyer and football commentator of having leanings towards Rangers, whereas Jock always protested he was a Hamilton Accies man. Well, whatever his leanings I was trying to avoid showing mine.

Jock was my boss and I have always found it wise to keep on the good side of the boss. Whatever my true feelings. If the truth be told Jock Brown had awarded me a contract to be Chief Scout and it was pitiful; it was embarrassing. Davie Hay had gone by then to take Celtic to court after failing to settle as Jock's assistant. Davie had been earning a healthy whack in the Chief Scout job, later revealed to be £65,000 a year, but what I was offered was pitiable for a club of Celtic's standing. I had committed myself to that club and they wanted me to stay but they offered me a fraction of Davie's salary.

The basic deal was £300 a week. To save you doing the maths, that worked out at £15,000 a year – before tax.

Ask anyone on the street what they think the backroom staff at Celtic would have been on at that time and you would have heard crazy figures.

They would have been guessing in excess of £100,000 a man with a company car thrown in.

The more sensible supporter would maybe lower his estimation to £40,000 a year.

I had been informed, after all, that my opposite number at Rangers was earning in the region of £42,000 at the time.

What I was given, then, was an insulting deal, which I nevertheless accepted because I wanted to be part of Celtic. Self-respect is never a consideration when the bills printed in red ink are lying behind the door.

To me £15,000 to work for Celtic doing a job I loved was still better than earning slightly more as a chemical salesman or a gas metre reader – jobs I have done in my time I should add.

I was travelling the world watching football and there are people out there who would do that for nothing to serve Celtic.

Only, however, if they have no mortgage, kids and bills piling up. And I had all of the above.

I was never in any doubt that I was probably the worst paid chief scout at a major European club ever.

There were admin staff at Parkhead probably earning double what I was being paid to discover the club's next big thing.

I knew what other men in the same post at clubs nowhere near the size of Celtic were paying their chief scouts. And I would never be arrogant enough to suggest I deserved more than them. But in no way was I any worse – unless you witnessed the figures on my payslip every month.

Jock Brown thought he was the great negotiator. Wim and others saw it otherwise. By the end so did I.

So both men disappointed me. Wim did not fight hard enough for that job. Nowhere near as hard as Tommy Burns had the year before in the quest to keep his head above water.

Tommy was making himself unwell and had to surrender in the end. That was never the case with Wim. He gave up on it too easy. After winning the League he could have named his terms and held Fergus over a barrel, he could have changed it all. Not many got the better of the little man who owned the club, but Wim Jansen had just stopped Rangers rampaging over the Scottish landscape after nine years of unassailed dominance. He held the whip hand with the paying customer.

He clearly decided it was not worth the hassle. Maybe the job made him feel unwell, I do not know. But I felt he gave up too early and I was sad about that because by the time he left I was enjoying the football side of working with him.

When he eventually said enough was enough in the Palacio Hotel, Estoril 48 hours after the League was won on the final day and Rangers had been stopped dead, the recriminations were long and weary. And I already knew this much; the new man would have to toe the line – or else.

Chapter Fifteen

Flying Without Wings

I HAVE SPENT a life terrified of flying. Terrified. And yet long after my playing career was over I spent years as a scout at major football clubs, including Celtic, flying all over the world.

These days I can take a pill to help me cope. At Celtic the plane would hardly be 300ft off the ground at Glasgow Airport on the 5.55am red eye to Amsterdam and I was out of it, pissed drunk.

I would have been drinking the night before. Then I would get up and scramble my way to the check-in desk half cut.

The plane would just be taking off when I would have an itchy finger and up it would go to attract an air attendant's attention. I needed a drink and it would be the first thing she brought out.

If I was travelling first class with Celtic it would be champagne and orange juice. If I was flying economy I would be less choosy.

It never affected my work – or so I told myself – because I would always leave home as early as possible for a journey. Better to travel than to arrive they say. Not for me guv'nor, not for me.

I would take an early flight deliberately so I could arrive somewhere with time to sober up. If there was an evening game to watch in Holland I would get myself to Amsterdam or wherever for two o'clock in the afternoon.

Some people would use that time to go shopping and buy nice presents for the wife and family. Perfume dear? A computer game son? Not for the Ritchies. Retail was no form of therapy for what I was suffering.

I was in my bed recovering from what I had drunk to get through the flight.

The game would be an 8pm kick-off. And I would grab whatever recovery I could from the drink in the morning, before a bite to eat to soak up the alcohol.

I suppose that could impact on your work. But to me watching football used to be similar to the culture that surrounded drinking and driving 25 years ago.

Everyone thought back then they were a better driver drunk. That their hand to eye co-ordination was that bit better with some Dutch courage in them. Steadies the hand they would say. Listen, I know fine the two examples are not the same – no one ever killed a footballer by watching him drunk. If they did there would not be a football player alive in the whole of

Glasgow. Let's just say I once felt a bit more forceful about a player with a wee warmer inside me. A bit more confident of my judgement.

It used to be that in the good old days when 70,000 would turn up for an Old Firm game and 69,500 would have a skinful inside them. That's the culture we came from. I did not need the drink to be a football scout. I never had some irresistible compulsion to drink before a game. It was the flight I was blotting out, not life itself.

Besides, things are different now, I do not feel the need to drink to blank out the fear of the wings falling off.

I take medication to help me conquer turbulent skies without the need for an alcoholic high. Twenty years ago my drug for coping was also medicinal, but you did not get what I was knocking back on the National Health Service.

Not long after I went back to Celtic as a scout Tommy Burns sent me down to the English League Play-offs at Wembley.

I said, 'fine.' I thought I would be going by train. But Thomas, as I knew him, told me he had already arranged to book tickets for me so I could travel down by air.

I mulled this over, then two days later plucked up the courage to go in and summon up an excuse or two. The wife was ill; the boys were acting up, the usual stuff. I cannot even remember what I tried, it was pointless, an exercise in whistling in the wind.

'It's all booked,' said Tommy. 'Everything's there on the desk.'

So just as I was due to go I contracted a mysterious stomach bug. That old favourite of the Monday morning desperado. Was I actually ill? Take a wild guess.

I was desperate to get down there, desperate to see the games, desperate to discover the next big thing for Celtic.

Neil Lennon, who would go on to become one of Martin O'Neill's key lieutenants at Celtic after signing in a £6 million deal in 2000, was one of the players I wanted to cast an eye over at Crewe. Danny Murphy, who would join Liverpool and Charlton, another.

But my desperation to avoid flying outweighed all of that. It overrode the needs of my employer, my colleagues, my family and dependents.

This was me. This was big Andy Ritchie, the big easy-going guy who cared for nothing. The international talent spotter who could not fly. You could not make it up. But excuses? I made up plenty of them.

It was classic avoidance. I was using any strategy I could to offset being rumbled. I did a lot of that.

I'm not the only man who has ever worn a Celtic jersey with a fear of flying. The late, great Jimmy Johnstone lived alongside me in Uddingston before he passed away with Motor Neurone Disease. They will never make another Jimmy Johnstone – a little dynamo of a man voted the greatest Celt ever. And legend has it that the little maestro would do anything to avoid flying. So much so that Jock Stein once promised him he would not have to fly to Belgrade for the second leg of a European Cup game if he did the business at Parkhead in the first game. The wee fella scored two and set up three that night. Fear has its uses; there is no drug or steroid with that kind of power.

And yet it seemed to me that every time there was a Lisbon Lion event on in America or Australia Jinky would make it. If you had said to me in his shoes, 'fancy a free trip to America? A fortnight in Florida with Celtic supporters standing the drinks?' then you would be wasting your time. Believe me, if it took me an hour, a day or a week I would find an excuse to give it a miss.

Chapter Sixteen

Doctor No

DOCTOR Josef Venglos arrived to headlines, which made Wim Jansen's arrival resemble the Second Coming. It was not so much Dr Jo, as 'Dr Who?'

The man was 62 and many felt his best years were behind him. He was a lovely man Dr Jo and I could well imagine him being my own granddad when he rolled up in a grey suit, Celtic scarf rather awkwardly draped around his neck.

And yet misplaced loyalty to a man with an unashamedly avuncular air cost me my job. Just as in the Wim Jansen season I would learn well before the end of the League campaign that change was in the air. I was placed in a devil and deep blue sea situation. And this time I would not survive the cull.

On reflection it should have been clear to me that I was backing the wrong horse.

Dr Jo came to Celtic at a time when the fight and guile, which made him a respected figure in world football had gone. His last visit to Parkhead had been for a 5–0 thrashing with Sporting Lisbon in a UEFA Cup game and he had been a disaster at Aston Villa. To most people he was a bizarre appointment, but not to me. To those who ran the club he fitted the bill perfectly because he was controllable and easily influenced, a man who had ceased saying 'no' many years before.

And yet even after being worn down by his years at the top level he still had not experienced anything like Celtic.

The Dr Jo who turned up in the old-fashioned jacket and shiny shoes that day was not the same Dr Jo who walked out the door 12 months later. If he was not a grandfather when he walked into Celtic Park then he certainly became one before he left minus a trophy to his name.

When the former Czech national coach left Glasgow he was on medication for the stresses of life at Celtic. How do I know that? Because I saw him take it.

And that was at a time when he was more than willing to toe the party line being laid down from on high by Fergus and Jock.

The pressures of trying to do the job were becoming unbearable to the old fella. Strange things were beginning to happen on the training ground and that was when the players began to realize all was not well.

He would try out odd manoeuvres involving three wingers attacking down the flanks, before throwing in crosses for three strikers to attack. And there was only one goalkeeper to save them. The balls were raining into the net like nobody's business and the poor keeper was being left a nervous wreck. It was like a scene from the old Bill Forsyth movie Gregory's Girl.

One or two of us would go along to watch this and leave thinking, 'geez, old Jo has lost the plot here'.

The players knew there was a major problem. Authority was draining away from the coaching staff because the team were smelling the fear and the desperation of the main man.

Players are the best gauge of how a club is going in their demeanour and their performances. A lot of modern players are incapable of articulating anything.

But I used to speak privately to Paul Lambert, who would go on to manage Livingston and Wycombe Wanderers before taking Norwich up to the Premiership and moving to Aston Villa. Paul was a player who always showed tremendous respect for whoever he worked for, striking up superb relationships with Ottmar Hitzfeld and Martin O'Neill before he retired. Yet he would tell me frankly; it just was not happening for Josef. It just was not there.

These days people remember the old boy fondly for his talk of 'sportive combinations' and for bringing the incomparable Lubomir Moravcik to the club.

Derided as an over-the-hill journeyman past his best in the press Lubo actually cost far less than the £300,000 reported at the time. And yet when he dismantled Dick Advocaat's Rangers in an incredible 5–1 thrashing in November 1998, scoring twice on his Old Firm debut, it was a rare highlight of an otherwise forgettable season.

Lubo was Josef's Celtic legacy. That perhaps plus the signature of Johan Mjallby from AIK Stockholm, a deal I worked hard to conclude.

And then there was Mark Viduka.

Like most of the best players Viduka came to light on a videotape and ended up at the centre of one of the more bizarre episodes of my time in football.

Before signing him I saw the tapes and spoke to people and made enquiries. I spoke to a fellow called Tommy Langley, an ex-Chelsea and Crystal Palace player who was the representative of Hilfa – the management company pitching the player to Celtic.

Because he had been involved in a deal to bring Paul Lambert back from Borussia Dortmund he was also able to tell me that Dortmund were interested in Viduka.

Michael Maier, Borussia's general manager, later told people in Germany that if Viduka had even a yard of pace he would have signed him immediately. Fortunately for Celtic – and for me – he did not.

Dr Jo Venglos had been asking me about players who might be able to take some of the burden and pressure from Henrik Larsson's shoulders.

He would not be the first Celtic coach to want that and far from the last either.

We needed someone to go in there with the ability and physical strength to share the load with Henrik.

I had fancied a Mexican international called Luis Hernandez, who had a similar style to Henrik. He had a decent World Cup in France 1998. But on doing some digging and seeking out reports I discovered that Hernandez had what might be called 'issues' you would not necessarily want in a Celtic dressing room.

So I spoke to Dr Jo about Viduka. What quickly became clear was that the money was not there at that point. Or, if it was, they were not releasing it.

So in he went to the 'pending tray'. He was my number one choice but I had to face the possibility that he might be another name with a red line through it.

Then came the divine intervention I needed when Celtic were drawn against Croatia Zagreb in a Champions League qualifier.

There was very little fortunate about the games themselves.

The club had waited a long, long time for a crack at the Champions League and the outcome was dismal.

Darren Jackson scored the goal at Parkhead which earned a 1–0 lead to take to Zagreb from the first leg, but in the intimidating surroundings of the Maksimir Stadium Viduka was key to a 3–0 destruction for the home team. It was three going on five. I swear I saw Dr Jo age another year or two that night.

But one good thing came of it all when Celtic became genuinely interested in Viduka. And that suited me fine. I had done all the homework; I knew he would cost £3 million, how much the player wanted and what he liked for breakfast.

My problem had always been convincing Dr Jo that Viduka was the right man. The game in Zagreb took care of that.

Jozef spoke to our central-defenders Marc Rieper and Alan Stubbs after the game and they were unanimous in their verdict.

Viduka was a real handful, a hell of a player. A tough guy with the strength of three men who gave them a hell of a bruising night.

Ditto Silvio Maric, the strike partner who went to Newcastle for £5 million and did not exactly set the heather alight. Frankly, I would have taken the two of them.

As it happened there was only money in the kitty for one of them and Celtic were only asking me about Viduka.

So what should have been the start of Celtic's Champions League journey against Croatia Zagreb had brought me significantly closer to the end of a journey I had embarked upon to put the big fellow in a green and white jersey.

After being taken apart by Viduka in Zagreb, Fergus McCann suddenly found the money to sign him. He had seen the evidence for himself. As I used to say to the coaches I worked with, I would have been better taking wee Fergus to scout the players with me than them. He was the power in the place.

As we quickly discovered, however, getting Viduka to put pen to paper was only the start of our problems. The start of an incredible problem in fact. For within 24 hours of arriving in Glasgow he had walked out.

There were all kinds of rumours flying around at the time about his mental health and so on. But the guy went on to play for Leeds and Middlesbrough and Newcastle and won countless caps for Australia. You do not do that if you are two cards short of a pack.

I still believe he was promised a large chunk of the cash at the Croatian end once he completed the move to Glasgow. By the time he reached Celtic it seemed the money was not available any more.

There were threats bouncing around all over the place and things were getting to him.

It was considerable sums of money involved and it was bugging the big guy. Suddenly he found himself in a position where he was not going to make as much money as he thought.

Furthermore he was stuck out at that big, remote hotel in East Kilbride that Celtic put all their new signings in.

He did not much like it and he thought to himself, 'stuff this, I'm off back to Australia'.

The mistake he made was not coming to speak to people at the club. But, then again, no one at Celtic made themselves available for that.

He had signed the contract and that was that. But as I used to joke at the time he had what might be called a 'Condor moment'.

Older readers will recall the cigar ad where everything would go wrong for some poor bugger and his only response was to sit back in realisation and strike up a Condor cigar. So it was with Mark Viduka. But instead of lighting a cigar, he bought a plane ticket and headed home to Melbourne.

He clearly felt he had not done the best thing joining in the first place. But it was too late for that; he was already a Celtic player.

Around that time I was speaking to his agent Bernie Mandic at crazy times of the night and told him Celtic were not about to let £3 million go up in smoke.

I had to speak to Mark and quickly. The club had told me I might have to fly out there and bring him back to Scotland.

I was no fan of flying at the best of times, so I did not fancy that one jot. Thankfully I finally got him on the phone and warned him there was no bluffing at play.

Wee Fergus McCann was ready to take it all the way and put him out of football. He was a young man, but he was not a stupid one. He realised he had made a mistake.

I gave him a straight choice; come over, score 25 goals for Celtic, get a move to England and everyone ends up a winner. Or stay in Melbourne and see his career rot in hell.

Two days later I got the call to say he was on his way back. As with the Three Amigos we were back in the sick pup market and we made the best out of a bad situation.

We got him a house and got him fit. And in the process got ourselves another decent signing under Dr Jo's stewardship.

The rest? It was close to being a bleeding disaster if the truth be told. The football department was a rudderless ship.

Dr Jo brought the Norwegian international Vidar Riseth in, or so the records show. But the truth is that Jock Brown did the business with his Austrian club LASK Linz before a bizarre business where the transfer money apparently disappeared at the other end after the deal was done. To my knowledge that was nothing to do with anyone at Celtic.

Of more importance was the fact that neither Jozef the head coach or I, the chief scout, had ever watched Vidar Riseth play. He had played for Norway against Scotland in France 98 and there were people in the Scotland set-up who knew about him. But not us.

Where, suddenly, had the policy of watching a player six times before signing him suddenly disappeared to?

I certainly never cast eyes on him – and it was in the dictat handed down from the boardroom that as Chief Scout I had to do so as an imperative.

The only conclusion to be reached from that was that the 'six-times' rule was only to be used as a stick to beat the football department with. When Vidar Riseth came in for £900,000 without so much as a nod from the management team it did not seem to matter so much.

Little wonder then that, despite a 5–1 reverse at Parkhead in November 1998, little Dick Advocaat proceeded to run rings round his alleged rivals. Rangers, with Brian Laudrup imperious, won the domestic treble in 1998–99 by a country mile. Celtic were in absolute disarray – and had been now for some time.

Under Tommy and Wim the patient had seemed to be making a recovery as the vast new stands of Celtic Park took shape on the Parkhead skyline.

But those stands were built on poisoned foundations. The club had relapsed into intensive care.

And unbeknown to me the search for a cure had already commenced under Allan MacDonald, the new Chief Executive appointed to run the club as soon as Fergus McCann kept his agreement to sell his shares and sail off into the sunset with £40 million in his back pocket. With catastrophic consequences for yours truly as it transpired.

Chapter Seventeen

The King is in the Building

TOWARDS the end of Dr Jo Venglos' inglorious season in charge Monica, Celtic's one-time trusty receptionist, placed a call to my office.

'Andy, I've got the King on the phone for you.'

'Monica,' I said laughing, 'Elvis is dead, step away from the chip shop.'

A lovely, yet formidable, woman when crossed, Celtic's receptionist was in no mood for humour. 'No, Andy,' she scolded, 'Kenny Dalglish is on the phone.'

I still thought it was some kind of joke. Cautiously I said to her to put my old teammate through. To say curiosity was in danger of killing the cat would be putting it politely. I had read all the talk of the rock star Jim Kerr of Simple Minds bringing Kenny into a consortium to buy the club on condition that Fergus renounce his vast pay-off and sell up. But this was unexpected.

My perception of the conversation may have blurred with the passing years but as I recall it went something along the following lines.

'Andy,' came Kenny's unmistakably gruff tones. 'You're the Chief Scout aye?'

When I replied in the affirmative an order was barked out with what I can only describe as near military precision.

'Get yourself down to Newcastle this weekend. Nikos Dabizas and Nobby Solano are available. Get the two of them sorted out. Go down and get the wheels in motion right now.'

To be clear, Dabizas and Solano were never on any scouting list at Celtic Park prior to that. I knew of both players, of course. But their names had never cropped up in any conversation I had with a head coach.

To say I was bemused would be putting it politely. This was not a request – I formed the distinct impression I was being told. And all this from a man who, whatever the rumours, still had no official role at Celtic Football Club.

I said to him, 'Kenny, what normally happens here is that I run these things past the manager and chairman here. Are they available for decent money?'

There was a pause. I felt he was in no mood for discussing the matter.

'Never mind that,' was the jist of the reply. 'It doesn't matter, just get down there and get it moving.'

I tried reasoning once more.

'Kenny, what I do is go in and see Dr Jo and Eric and if they are happy with that then I go down for a look.'

Again, the response was dismissive.

'Never mind that, just get down there for a look. Do you not want to do your job or something?' he added, only half in jest I felt. 'Never mind mucking about.'

And so I hung up with a promise to phone Kenny back the next week with news of my top-secret mission. So secret that I wondered just who else knew what was now seemed to be apparent to me; Kenny Dalglish was coming back to Celtic.

On the Friday afternoon the players had all gone when I popped my head round the door to see Dr Jo and Eric sitting with a pot of tea.

'Can I have a quick five minutes gents?' I asked. They invited me to take a seat.

'Listen, I am going to ask you a question. I read in the paper about Jim Kerr coming in and Kenny coming in. Just tell me this, is Kenny Dalglish coming back here?'

What I witnessed then was the body language equivalent of a mirror, brake and handbrake manoeuvre. There was an uncomfortable shuffling. I gained the distinct impression that this was not entirely a shock to them. They did not throw their arms up in the air and begin screaming 'woe is me'. I could be wrong of course; they may just have been speechless.

In any case I told them about the phone call and outlined my dilemma. These men were my line managers and yet Kenny Dalglish was giving me orders.

'I have to ask you gentleman. What do I do about this? Do I go to Newcastle tomorrow? Please tell me because I am in a position here and I only want to do my job.

'I like this job and I don't want to lose it. I think I'm alright at it and I want to keep it. What do I do about this? My job is to do deals through you Josef and I'm asking you and Eric.'

The response was cautious and guarded. 'Leave it with us' was the gist of their response. I was none the wiser and frankly I was a worried man.

I came out and, in a fatal miscalculation; I did not go to Newcastle. I spent the day elsewhere. Big mistake.

I felt I was doing the right thing because throughout my time at Celtic I had always had to explain to the head coach alone where I was going and why.

It was not in my remit as Celtic's chief scout to phone up Cambuslang Travel and book a ticket to Rio De Janeiro to watch Ronaldo. The head coach had to authorise every scouting trip verbally.

I put my faith in their advice to avoid Newcastle because that was the deal I made; I worked to the contract I was given. Doing my own thing would have been a blatant breach.

Now, of course, I see that I should have done just that. Had they told me on the QT that Kenny Dalglish was definitely coming in as Director of Football at the end of that season with John Barnes as his head coach I would have been sipping Newcastle Brown Ale in a bar adjacent to St James' Park before you could say, 'Way-ay man'.

In retrospect I wish I had said, 'fuck Dr Jo and Eric Black'. Not least given Eric's emergence as number two to the aforementioned Barnes in the so-called 'Dream Team' signed up by the new Chief Exec Allan Macdonald.

But I was only doing what I had done with Thomas, what I had done with Wim. Now I was in devil or deep blue sea situation.

Eventually Josef and Eric came back to me on the Monday or Tuesday and said to me; 'Don't worry about what happened last week. Forget it.'

'But what do I do when I have to phone Kenny back and say we want nothing to do with the Newcastle players?' I asked.

'It will be fine,' came the reply. 'Don't worry.'

That was easy for them to say of course. They did not have to phone the greatest Scottish player to grace a dark blue jersey, a legendary figure and tell him we were effectively turning a rubber ear to his wishes.

When I made the call it was a brief conversation. I phoned Kenny and told him Celtic wanted nothing to do with the players in question. That Dr Jo and Eric had not wanted me to go to Newcastle.

I do not think I even got that far. The unmistakable sound of a dialling tone was the immediate response. I thought there was a fault on the line. There was not.

Now I had good cause to be worried. Dr Jo's departure looked increasingly inevitable and when the old man left the new guard was spearheaded by one Kenneth Mathieson Dalglish esq.

Our one and only conversation on his appointment as Director of Football was even shorter than the telephone call I had made weeks before. It was all of 10 seconds long.

My perception was that he avoided speaking to me every time I went up the stairs to the administration block in the Jock Stein Stand where he had a large office.

I felt a grave sense of injustice because it was clear what was coming; and so far as I was concerned I was an innocent man. I might have been a young teammate of Kenny's under Jock Stein but things had moved on. The old loyalties counted for nothing now.

There was no longer the bond that existed between two young boys making their way in a dressing room full of old pros. If I think about it now it might be that Kenny had been trying to do me a favour all along with that phone call; one I failed to take advantage of.

His view might have been that he had told me what to do and that I was not up to the job.

'I told him what to do and he cannae blinking well do it,' might have been the view adopted when I was drummed out of the tent. Terry McDermott, who arrived as 'Social Convenor' at least did what he was told.

Eric Black, I would later come to believe, had also been summoned to Allan MacDonald's place in Edinburgh to be briefed on what was happening. So it's feasible, in my view, to think that he might also have known what was happening.

But it disappointed me that no one in the know ever shut the office door, put the kettle on and explained to me what was going on. I was left in limbo. Totally, completely and unfailingly. And that was what finished me off.

Listen, maybe my old colleague did not want to be the bearer of bad news and he always planned to bin me anyway. The Solano and Dabizas exchange might have been a smokescreen.

But had I done what Kenny had told me I might have been well in with the new regime. At the very least I would have hung on longer than they did; a disastrous and shameful defeat to Inverness Caledonian Thistle in the Scottish Cup providing conclusive proof that the rookie coach Barnes had lost the dressing room after just seven months in charge.

It gave me no satisfaction to note that Barnes would face the same fate as me the very next day; a cursory dismissal. You do not wish that on anyone. Naturally, Kenny hung on for a bit until Martin O'Neill's eventual arrival in the summer of 2000.

But I knew my fate was sealed the day I went down to Portsmouth to take in a game against West Ham along with my agent friend Tommy Langley.

West Ham manager Harry Redknapp was driving into the car park when he rolled down his car window to speak to Tommy, who he knew from way back. I was introduced as Celtic chief scout and on shaking my hand Harry dropped a bombshell.

'I was doing a bit of business with Celtic today as it happened.'

'Really?' I asked. 'What was that then?'

'They've signed Eyal Berkovic for £5 million.'

It was a horrible moment and I tried to disguise my bewilderment. There I was, chief scout of Celtic, and I knew nothing about one of the most expensive signings the club ever made. It was clear to me then what was coming.

I wondered later if I might have been dismissed as retribution for my verdict years earlier on Kenny's son Paul, a young kid at Celtic for a time.

As a scout I gave the opinion that he was not good enough to remain at the club in a meeting attended only by Tommy Burns, Billy Stark, David Hay and myself.

But the manager was also of the opinion that he would not be good enough as well, and Paul was subsequently released. When you consider that Tommy ended up returning to Celtic as Kenny's assistant and had served in the same role at Newcastle that theory simply does not add up for me.

So I am more inclined to go with my initial instinct. My failure to act on the Dabizas and Solano conversation had cost me the job I loved.

Naturally, there were other reasons offered.

I had a meeting with the chief executive Allan MacDonald where he put it to me I had been selling stories to the press. He claimed he had spoken to editors of major newspapers and that I had been flogging inside information for a profit. To me that was totally untrue and deeply wounding.

I felt worse about that than anything else that was said about me. If I had been taking £10,000 off the papers for sensitive information people would have had every right to call my morality into question. But it was never the case.

I did take calls from newspapers about players and transfers and if I knew nothing about a player I would deny it outright.

If I did know something then I stuck to a straight line of no comment. If I went silent at the end of the phone then the journalist in question knew they were not far off the mark with their information.

I told Allan MacDonald straight that I wanted him to bring the people accusing me of selling stories into Celtic Park to meet me face to face. I wanted my lawyer to come in and speak with these newspaper people allegedly making these suggestions. Oddly, that never happened.

Eventually MacDonald told me straight that Kenny just did not want me at Celtic Park.

I was not very happy about that and told him what I thought I had achieved in terms of bringing good players to the club.

I thought I did it reasonably well. But the response was to tell me that no one at Celtic Park seemed to know what I did.

At the end of it all he promised to go back to Kenny and do what he could to try and keep me at the club and would come back to me within a month.

At the end of that period I was called upstairs and told there was no change of heart from Kenny. He wanted to bring other people in.

I sat outside Kenny's office on three or four afternoons trying to talk to the man who was my teammate in my early years at the club. I would sit for hours and hours to no avail and I was getting angry and upset. But I never did get my audience.

Fergus McCann got plenty wrong in his time at Celtic but when he alone voiced concerns over the plans to bring Kenny back to the club he was once again showing an uncanny ability to foresee the future.

The 'Dream Team' as they were dubbed by the press did not last long.

John Barnes had never managed a club before and from an early stage it was clear he was struggling.

I knew a lot of the players and suffice to say, I knew all was not well in the dressing room. There was not a great deal of respect for the management team.

Craig Burley had gone with the team to Aberdeen for a game at Pittodrie and I was at Parkhead when they arrived back.

Burley was furious as I recall because he had not started and had only been put on the pitch for a few minutes at the end of the game.

Burley and Dalglish had a conversation in the corridor and it was no great surprise when the midfielder became a Derby County player not long after that.

What people do not know is that Martin O'Neill – a future Celtic manager – had called up asking about taking him to Leicester before that. Either way it was another deal where Celtic got their money back and then some.

It was not a great surprise to me when things subsequently ended badly for Barnes on an infamous night in February 2000. The surprise was that it was Inverness Caledonian Thistle who brought it all to a head when they toppled Celtic from the Scottish Cup.

The tales of Mark Viduka throwing off his boots and refusing to go out for the second half as the 'keeper Jonathan Gould pointed fingers at the £5 million man Eyal Berkovic made banner headlines across the globe.

It would be suffice to say that Kenny's period at Celtic was not one of his better episodes in football.

But neither did it do his immense reputation as a player or a legendary manager any lingering harm either. He's a wealthy man and is back at the Liverpool helm as manager for a second spell.

Me? I can hardly say the same.

At the time I was sacked it was a devastating blow. I was hurt and I was bewildered.

I never cried when I was transferred from Celtic in 1976, but I sure as hell cried when I lost the job as chief scout.

It was a job, which had come to me, not one I had gone looking for. And not long after I started doing it Tommy Burns said to me, 'Trumpton, you're good at this.'

When I look back at it now I was learning on the job. I spent a lot of time in there just talking to people, soaking up what was needed and trying to forge a plan.

I was never good with computer databases. All I wanted to do was watch football games.

And when I took over the job from David Hay as chief scout I only ever had one scout down in Liverpool at my disposal. These days Celtic employ guys in Belgium, Portugal, the Americas, wherever. All of them seeking out the next Emilio Izaguirre or Beram Kayal.

But in those days a guy called John Murphy was the sum and parts of my 'scouting network' after Jimmy Lumsden left to go with Tommy Burns to Reading. My reports and records were kept in a brown paper folder as high as a desk. I may not have been the most organised at times, but despite it all I think I was good at the job.

So when I lost it I remember breaking down in my kitchen in Viewpark. And that despite the fact I was pitifully paid. Believe me, I was never living the life of a lord.

The hassle and the nonsense, the politics and the flying were a source of grief and stress more than once. It is not an easy gig by any stretch. But, still, I cried when I lost that job and I am not ashamed to admit it.

When I joined Celtic as a 15-year-old kid I was a Motherwell supporter. Tommy Burns regarded Celtic Football Club as his beginning, his middle and his end, I did not. But by the time I walked through the glass doors at Celtic Park for the final time I had developed a deep and lasting affection for the place. I do not claim to be a born and bred Celtic man, that would be a nonsense. I grew up supporting Motherwell and the best years of my career were spent at Morton.

But by the time I left I was a Celtic man in every sense.

Chapter Eighteen

The Gambler

*MY FATHER was never a gambler. Nor my brother. Nor anybody
I grew up with.*

I was always interested in horses. But my dad always said the same thing about the equine race.

'They puke out of one end and they shit out the other, son. That's all you need to know.' I always took that as a warning.

By the time I laid eyes on my first betting slip, then, I was a young player at Celtic Park.

There were other guys doing it and peer pressure played its part. There were guys I used to travel with on the bus to reserve games and they would all have a bet on. Why not me?

At that time we finished training at 12 o'clock and we were paid cash on a Tuesday. At that time you had a simple choice; you either went for a pint or you went to the bookies and spent a couple of hours before dinner.

I cannot speak for anyone else, but that's how my problems started. With gambling at least.

Problem gambling never starts when you are skint. Ammunition is always required and as a young player at Celtic I was walking about with a pocket full of live artillery.

The bullets came in a pay packet every week and by God I fired them. I was no good with money back then and nothing has changed in the years since. Easy come, easy go.

As you do in life, you meet people. And I was meeting plenty of people who liked a bet.

Over the years I have acquired a fantastic interest in racehorses and horse racing in general.

Jockeys, trainers, the whole fucking shooting match. I can read the Racing Post from front to back, back to front and between every line.

I can't say precisely when the great interest in horse racing changed from being a hobby to being a serious problem. No gamber ever can. But, very clearly, it did.

In retrospect it started to become a problem around the age of 21. Why should I have recognised it was a problem? Because I was betting a week's wages within hours of receiving them.

I did not feel I had a problem, not at all. I was married to Rena, but why should I feel there was a problem when all I had to do was drop into the Airdrie Savings Bank and withdraw a sum of money equivalent to my wages?

I did that many times, too many times to mention. I had odds and ends of cash tucked away at that time and it was my safety net.

I covered my tracks, as every gambler learns to do. I never worried, because there was another week's wages around the corner. And, anyway, every gambler knows his next win is just around the corner. It's just a matter of when.

Take a problem gambler and you can magnify that sentiment by a thousand times.

And, believe me, in any football dressing room you will find every kind of gambler imaginable.

To this day you could walk into any bookies in the West of Scotland and find a guy you have either played with or against. Put spare money and spare time together and that is what you get.

Back then it was the norm. There was no such thing as problem gambling.

These days you cannot pick up a paper without reading some sanctimonious lecture on how to spot the gambler in your midst. In those days everyone was at it.

Bit by bit my punting grew. I started small, with a tenner here and there. If I did not have it I borrowed it. And I did not care who from.

That is just what a problem gambler does. He runs out of his own money and when that is gone he needs more. A soldier cannot fight without bombs. And I was that soldier.

By the time I bought a Mercedes from former Radio Clyde Mr Abie I was moving towards a dangerous place.

It was a 180S and I remember getting a decent deal on it, it was a beautiful car.

But I sold it six months later to a guy in Stirling for more money. I got there, collected the cash and was skint 24 hours later. I had punted the lot. We were talking £6,000 – a lot of money at that time.

Why did I do it? I needed the money, simple. I needed to pay back wages I had spent and friends I had borrowed money from.

I used some to take the heat off my creditors and the plan was to keep some back to buy another car. Naturally I needed a small slice of the cash to back the next winner as well. And so, within hours, it was gone. And so was my lovely car.

When the cash ran out and friends could not oblige I would borrow from institutions and banks. Money was easy to obtain then.

I was a relatively well-known figure in Scottish football. Borrowing money was the last of my problems. Paying it back the first.

I would turn up for games after a hellish week of robbing Peter to pay Paul. But I was lucky in one regard. There would be people biting my backside for their money back, but as soon as five to three came about it was all gone.

I would shower, shave, slap on some aftershave and have a pint to forget. But when I woke up again on Sunday morning it was all back on my shoulders like a lead weight. Sunday was never Saturday.

I learned to adapt to that kind of lifestyle. But many was the night I went to bed a worried man, telling myself I had to win a few quid the next day to put it all right.

'Tomorrow has to be better,' was my motto.

Rena and I bought a new home in Mossend to celebrate signing a four-year deal at Morton. At that time I put quite a substantial sum of money down on the house. But within 18 months we had to sell it to pay off my gambling debts.

We could not afford it any longer and were not paying the mortgage. We fell behind and got out.

We moved back in with my mother-in-law. At the time I did not regard it as any great betrayal or anything.

I was just glad to get the pressure off by selling the house and having no one chasing us for money any more.

What can I say? I was immature beyond words. I played for Celtic's first team at 16. I had the body of a man and the mind of a boy.

When we lost the house and stayed with Rena's mother for a bit we moved to Mount Vernon in Glasgow, then down to London when I quit football and got the job at the Barbican.

Had I learned any lessons? Not so you would notice.

I remember driving back up to Scotland from London for a few days and en route I noticed there was a race meeting on at Leicester.

So off I went to the races for a day. And no matter how hard I tried I could not lose.

Anyone who bets will recognise that as something, which happens as often as a blue moon.

I was gambling on the races at Leicester and heading to the on course bookies in between races to see what other meetings I could punt on.

It was freezing cold when I leapt back in the car and encountered awful driving conditions. It was a terrible night, cats and dogs.

I thought, 'stuff it' so I cut across to Blackpool and decided to make the rest of the journey in the morning.

I booked into a nice big sea front hotel and emptied everything onto the bed. It was 1985. I had started my journey with £80 in my pocket and by the time I counted it out I had £6,500 in notes and coins scattered all around me.

I had won every penny at Leicester and I have never forgotten the name of the horse that got me on my way that day.

It was called One to Mark and I picked it because my oldest son's name is Mark and to me it was an omen.

The trainer was Pipe and the jockey was Peter Scudamore and it romped in at 25/1. I had £25 on that horse and within minutes I felt I could do no wrong.

I actually bet my last winner when it was dark and I was in the bookies gazing out at a bleak scene. I had £400 at 5/2 on the last winner at Windsor and such was my form that the bookie was reluctant to take it. Eventually he relented and I finished up with £1,000 in my hand at Leicester Race Course thanks to a horse running miles away at Windsor.

I was the last man standing. Me and the bookmaker.

Later, in my Blackpool hotel room I packed the money into my pocket – I was not leaving that kind of money lying around – and had a drink at the bar downstairs.

I had a sandwich and cup of coffee and stepped outside for a breath of air. I almost went back in, so horrendous was the weather.

But as I was smoking a cigarette a fellow walks past trailing two greyhounds on leads.

I pipes up to him, 'where you taking them?'

He says to me, 'the greyhound racing at Bloomfield Road.'

So off I went believing I was having the kind of day when fortune truly was favouring the brave.

I was wrong. You've heard the phrase one man and his dog. Well, I must have been one of just four spectators that night, but it did not stop me losing £1,000.

I returned to the room consoling myself with the thought I would still have £5,500 when I set off for Scotland the next morning.

Some consolation. After a brief four-day break up the road I had to borrow £60 from my poor mother-in-law to get petrol for the drive back down to London. I had blown the lot. It was gone.

I sent the £60 back up the road, and it was around then I began to realise I might have a problem.

If anything that day at Leicester made me want to keep betting. I had done it once and I wanted it again. Badly.

But it was beginning to hurt the people around me and I had to take notice of that eventually.

If the truth be told I had known for some time I was in trouble, but I was in denial. Most gamblers are.

For the most part I only truly recognised it as a problem during times of crisis. Crisis is when you have punted money you should not have because it belonged to someone else. And I was doing that far too often.

It all came to a head when I went to Barclays Bank and borrowed £4,500. I told them I needed the money to put a nice new kitchen and bathroom in our place at the Barbican.

It was a lie. I did not even own the property.

So Barclays gave me £4,500 and I gambled the lot. Every last penny.

Which was a problem, because like all banks Barclays wanted their money back. And I no longer had it. What I did have was a major problem.

I had no choice. I declared myself to my wife and admitted I had a problem. I was leaping from one catastrophe to the next. The problem was that the length of time between the catastrophes was becoming shorter and shorter.

I was in serious danger of losing my job. Yet I was already losing the wages to gambling anyway.

I went to a Gamblers Anonymous meeting in Shoreditch in London. It was held in a horrible, grotesque hall. It was filthy and unpleasant.

And all I saw when I looked around me were what I perceived to be down and outs. Poor losers with a problem. I was not in their boat.

I did not feel comfortable. I did not belong with these people. I had problems, but nothing on their score.

When I had declared myself to my family there were tears and much gnashing of teeth. Everyone agreed I had a problem. But this? This was not me.

They handed me a filthy, watery cup of tea and sitting staring at that cup I managed to avoid my own reflection staring back. I was kidding myself on.

Barclays Bank? Losing my wages? Losing my job? Stuff all that.

I stayed 10 minutes and I was out of there. Did I need this place? To be sitting there with these down and out losers? Did I fuck.

It was the same arrogance and attitude, which had cost me my playing career. I got out of there and headed for a local pub for a pint to kill time. I was not that daft.

When the time was right I headed home and told Rena what she wanted to hear. I had learned a lot, I was back on the path to redemption.

I came to an agreement with my wife and my employers to pay Barclays back and that took the pressure off. It fooled me into thinking everything would be fine.

I stayed off the gambling for a couple of weeks. I told myself that was all I needed.

When you are a problem gambler a couple of weeks without a bet feels like a year.

When the fortnight was up I eased my way back in with small stakes. And off I went again.

It's a condition, which is progressive in its nature. That is how it works.

You are never truly clear of it and it will creep up on you like a clinging ivy.

So there I was back gambling as much as ever. And I did not agree to seek help again until we were back living in Scotland some time around 1990.

I was doing all sorts of sums of money by then, anything I could get my hands on. And by now I was mixing it with another evil concoction to make one hell of a cocktail; alcohol.

I was drinking heavily and it mattered little what shoulder I turned to. There was a demon resting on each one.

It was really beginning to take its toll on me at that time. Towards the end of my time in London life had become turmoil for my whole family.

I had run my course in London. I was fine; I had plenty to occupy my time – and money – in London. But the family felt it might be best to opt for a return home and I could hardly argue.

Did anything change? Did the air blowing in from the Clyde make everything right? Did I see the error of my ways? Not so you would notice.

I drank and I gambled. I gambled and I drank.

I remember I did a load of money one time and felt completely unable to open the blinds for three days. I hid myself away, ashamed of what I had done. Yet again.

It was how I imagine a drug addict feels. I woke up every morning and wondered how I would get back in the game that day. How would I get the cash?

Things were really bad and I had a feeling of abject hopelessness. I was depressed.

I was not interested in betting a tenner each way on a horse at even money. That was no good to me.

I needed big money and that was where the hopelessness and the depression set in. I had no conceivable means of making that kind of money. And yet I needed it. How I needed it.

I remember sitting in the house feeling completely unable to move. All I could hear was Rena imploring me to get some help.

Then, out of the blue, a guy phoned me. I had no idea who he was, but he knew all about my problems and me.

I accused Rena the minute I put the phone down and she admitted she had looked out a number for Gamblers Anonymous. She knew I would never phone him, so he phoned me instead.

I said I would phone him back. But instead he said he would phone me back in half an hour. And sure enough he did.

We had a chat and a long talk. That was on the Friday, I went to meet him on the Monday and discovered one of the best, most inspiring guys I have ever met in my life.

I cannot and will not name him. He would not want it. But I ended up in daily contact after that Monday meeting and for the next five years I did not lay a single bet. On anything.

I was attending three Gamblers Anonymous meetings a week and listening into the basic information and advice. I would sit beside Frank McGarvey, the former Celtic striker. But there were as many plumbers there as there were footballers.

For the first time in my life I was actually listening. And it felt good.

After a few weeks I felt physically and mentally better. I even got myself a job in Hillington.

I enjoyed the job and the company of the people I was working with. I was going out there and doing an honest day's work for an honest day's pay.

I was building my self-respect back up and we moved out of the house we were in and bought another one.

I enjoyed it, life was better. I cut back my drinking intake as well and my social life became healthier.

I got involved with Dukla Pumpherston, a pro celebrity charity football team, and worked hard until I took a call from an old mucker.

Jimmy Bone, a former Celtic and St Mirren player, had just landed the Saints manager's job and wanted me to go work with him. I was working all day and training boys all night.

I was filling my time, packing my days full. I was doing what they told me to do; leaving no space for gambling to fill the void. Without all that activity there would always be an enormous hole and I would only fill it by gambling. So I filled it in a positive and healthy way.

For once in my life I was doing what I was told by people who knew what they were talking about. I was keeping my nose clean.

I can still remember the day I placed my first bet at the end of the five years. David Cooper, the former Rangers and Scotland winger, had died just a couple of days before and I went to his funeral.

I met some old football pals there and they were heading to Hamilton Races a couple of days later. Would I like to come along?

I met up with them and I was back in the game. How did I feel after that? Terrible. I knew what I had done.

I went back to GA a couple of times again, ducking in and out half-heartedly.

I knew it worked – but for some reason I could not work up the same adrenalin and enthusiasm I had savoured for the five years previous. I felt I had let myself down.

Getting all this down now it does not feel as if I ever enjoyed the gambling much. But it seemed as if I did at the time. I loved it and hated it. It was a wife and a mistress.

I enjoyed reading the racing pages and I devoured them. I got to know a lot of people in the industry. These days I tell myself the gambling is under control. To a certain extent. But you never say never.

You are only a hair's breadth away from your next crisis. But it is only dangerous when you have a pocket full of money. And it is some time since I have been able to say that.

If I ever did have money again I would have other things to do with it now. I have a young granddaughter for a start. But that's not to say I would never have another bet.

I know too much to ever say that. It is never beaten.

Had I known when I was younger what I know now, however, it might never have become as bad as it did.

I would eventually put my extensive knowledge and experience of the whole subject to good use.

I was asked by big Tony Higgins and Fraser Wishart of the Scottish Professional Footballer's Association and by Andy Todd of the Renfrewshire Council of Addictions to go to Hampden and speak to a lot of young football professionals making their way in the game.

They were between 16 and 18 and in my eyes these kids will always be vulnerable.

As I said to them the only way to be sure they will never have a problem with gambling; the only way they can ever ensure it will not affect their career is to avoid betting from the outset.

There is never anything printed on your forehead, which says, 'problem drinker' or 'problem gambler'. We all look the same; we are all Jock Tamson's Bairns. Picking someone out with a problem then is no easy job. They can be well down a rocky road before help ever comes.

There's more help now than in my day, but you have to want the help first.

All you can ever say to these young boys, then, is 'don't start it.'

And if you have started it go and get help. If you've started and you do not think it is a problem make sure you go and get help.

Chapter Nineteen

South of the Border

It took me time to get over my departure from Celtic. Some men put a brave face on these things and pretend everything is fine. They jut out their chin and put on an appearance.

I will be honest, I was down and more than a bit depressed about it all. And I could not hide it.

I could not understand what I was supposed to have done wrong. It was hard to get back in the harness again.

Like most jobs in football, scouting is not something you get by sending off a CV and submitting an application. The jobs come up strictly via invitation.

And the truth is this. I did not know too many people in football in that time, but I was lucky because a lot of people seemed to know me.

I went to do some work for Barnsley. I met up with Dave 'Harry' Bassett, who was manager at the time and we went for a chat.

I did some work but to do the job properly I would have had to move south to Yorkshire and that was never for me. And if you are not living and breathing the club you work for it is hard to get a handle on it all.

In truth Harry never had the money to move me down there and that suited me fine. I had done a lot of European scouting and Harry wanted to break into that market.

So it would be suffice to say I did not make an enormous impact on Barnsley.

I took Gary Holt, the Scotland midfielder, from Kilmarnock down there. The club were doing alright, but I got the distinct impression from the off that it was never going to last.

It was never anything more than a stop-gap. A case of taking in a game to watch a player if I was not doing much that particular Saturday.

Harry was interesting to work with. He had his own ways of doing things and was his own man.

He might have been one of the last of the old brigade of managers. He wanted to control the whole situation; he wanted to have a firm command of the entire club.

But I never got involved in the actual everyday nuts and bolts of life there.

So much so that Harry actually had a word with John Gregory, then manager of Aston Villa, on my behalf.

I was introduced to John and we watched a game together. John wanted stuff done overseas and I signed up as Aston Villa's European Scout.

It was a lovely gig. Aston Villa is a fantastic club with a marvellous history and it felt like being back in the big time again for a bit.

The job came as a pleasant surprise and I spent a bit of time working with Ross McLaren, John's assistant at the time.

We would discuss things for hours at a time and it worked out well for a while. There was a lot of putting pens through names rather than circling them, travelling all over and keeping people up to date.

And I did some scouting of opponents when they were in the UEFA Cup one season.

It was interesting work, but it was not as involving or as satisfying as the job at Celtic had been.

It did not help that I was still working from Scotland, where I lived. I probably only saw Aston Villa play three times in that whole period. My job was to watch others play and report back.

The result of that was that I never had the day-to-day involvement or buzz of a top football club. At Celtic I used to love watching training every day. To me that was as enjoyable as the scouting. I absorbed everything about the club and I understood what was needed better as a result.

At Villa life felt like one long taxi ride to Glasgow Airport. I hated flying and would drink to make it easier.

And all of that contributed towards my alcohol intake creeping back up towards a dangerous level.

There was a lot going on in my head at that time. I was back on the old treadmill of early morning flights, drinking, then heading straight to bed in Brussels or wherever before getting up to watch a game at night.

I did that job for a couple of seasons before John Gregory left for Derby County – and I went with him.

Graham Taylor had joined Villa as a general manager in 2002 and I remember saying to Ross McLaren, 'there goes the next Aston Villa manager'.

Ross was dismissive saying, 'nah, he doesn't want that life any longer. He just wants to help out.'

But I found it impossible to believe the guy had come back unless the old chairman 'Dangerous' Doug Ellis had made him certain promises. Sure enough, five months later he was back in his second spell as manager of Aston Villa and I was working under him.

It's fair to say he and I were never a match made in heaven from the first day I went down for a meeting. I had never properly spoken to Graham and I travelled down there on a Saturday morning to watch Aston Villa's youth team play their Everton counterparts.

He knew who I was because he actually mentioned me in his book. I had played a pre-season game for Morton against Watford, as I mentioned earlier, and scored the goal of my life from the halfway line. This was a Watford team, remember, with the likes of Luther Blissett and John Barnes in their ranks.

Yet we thumped them 5–1 and we spoke a bit about my performance in that game.

We sat together in the stand and Wayne Rooney was playing for Everton. It was the first time I had seen him in the flesh and he was quite brilliant.

Afterwards I went down for a cup of tea with the new manager and he confided in me that he planned to sign Marcus Allback, the Swedish international striker.

There and then I knew we had a problem. I had seen Allback play for Heerenveen in Holland three or four times and my firm impression was that he simply was not good enough.

Heerenveen wanted £2 million for the guy, Villa were willing to pay it and I felt a distinct unease at this news. I told Graham straight that Allback was not good enough to play in the English Premier League and that he was nowhere near good enough to play for Aston Villa. It was my firm impression that he did not appreciate my input on the matter.

Maybe I should have bitten my tongue. But I could not very well go back on the opinion I had submitted in my reports to John Gregory. My view was there for all to see in black and white.

In a bid to see if I might have misjudged things I went out to see Allback play once more on the manager's instructions. This was my fifth time and I remember travelling with Martin Ferguson, the Manchester United scout and brother of Sir Alex. Needless to say he still was not good enough. Much as he had not been the first four times I had seen him.

So that was a bad start. As was his unhappiness with the money Aston Villa were paying me. It was an old story in essence. Graham wanted his own people scouting for him and I understood that.

I knew the game was well and truly up when he told me he was very much interested in signing a player called Ulises de la Cruz from Hibernian. Or as he was known to his detractors, 'Useless' de le Cruz.

He was an Ecuadorian international who had played one season in Edinburgh under Alex McLeish.

Taylor had seen him play in the 2002 World Cup while he was doing some television work and we had one or two discussions about the player's merits. Suffice to say I did not think he had any to speak of.

Again, I was perfectly blunt in my prognosis. Like Allback he was not good enough to play in the Premiership or for Aston Villa. That advice did nothing to prevent his arrival a short time later in an £850,000 deal.

By now word of my problems at Villa was spreading. John Gregory phoned me up and asked if I would like to join him at Derby on the same money I was earning at Villa Park. It was, as they say, a no brainer.

I went to speak to Graham Taylor to tell him I was moving and he did not put up any great fight. No fight at all, come to mention it.

So I made the move from one Midlands club to another and things seemed to have worked out.

Or so it appeared until six weeks into my new job when Derby ran into financial problems. The spectre of administration loomed and a new regime were coming in.

So, in all honesty, I can say I did the centre of a doughnut for Derby County. Even less, some might say.

They had no money to send me anywhere and no cash to sign players. All of which rendered the job of a football scout utterly pointless.

I was going through the motions of going to watch games in a vain quest to justify my existence. But, then again, football clubs are littered with a litany of people who never appear to contribute very much at all. I could live with it.

In the end my time at Derby probably only lasted about a year. By 2003 we were all out on our ear again and back to square one.

I drifted out of the game altogether and did some work for a chemical company. Basically I would pack a car full of products and tour Britain's glorious landscape trying to sell it. Things were not good.

They were worse than that, indeed. Things were becoming distinctly bad all round.

I had done that work before, but returning to it made me realise just how much football beats real work.

Being around any football club is exciting and invigorating. Being around a top club is the spice of life for me.

After leaving Derby I was asked to give evidence to the Football Corruption Enquiry headed up by Lord Stevens, the former head of the Metropolitan Police, in 2006.

They wanted to find out from me what had gone on when Aston Villa signed the Croatian player Bosko Balaban.

Someone said to me many years later that there were rumours of a lot of money sloshing round that deal for various parties. I can say quite categorically that none of it managed to find its way into the pocket of Andy Ritchie.

But in the midst of that whole deal there was a curious episode when Aston Villa had been drawn to play against NK Varteks of Croatia in the UEFA Cup and I was sent to compile a dossier on the opponents.

There were always perks to being a European scout. First-class hotels, seeing some of the continent's finest cities, a nice expenses tab. But this was a job with what might euphemistically be called 'extra' perks. Perks with long legs and some impressive female wiles.

And I was not the one doing the ordering, I felt as if I was actually being ordered to participate. There were girls and recreational substances being sent up to the room I had been assigned. Or perhaps I should say, the suite.

I remember thinking to myself this was not right. But did I feel bad? Did I hell. A couple of hours of what they were providing would have brought a smile to Jack Dee's face. It was a strange, strange business.

But ultimately there was little I could tell the enquiry because I had come into contact with none of the money they were chasing. I was not in the mix. All I had were suspicions based on anecdotal evidence. There was no smoking gun I could point at anyone.

By that time I had my own problems in any case. I was out of football altogether and I felt lost. I felt frustrated because I felt detached from the game I loved.

Add in a failed marriage and problems at home and it seemed as if I was being embroiled in the perfect storm. I was learning about terrible things that had happened within my own family.

I felt I was being attacked from all sides at that time and, to be frank, I could not understand why. I might be deluded here, but I felt I had not done a great deal wrong to deserve all of that.

In fact, for once in my life, I was trying to do a lot more right.

I had a problem with drink because my private life was spiralling out of control.

It was an absolute nightmare time for me and I made a lot of bad decisions financially. In terms of property and giving away cars and so on.

The truth was that by then I did not give a fuck about anything any longer.

I was in a bad way and I had lost my bearings. I cannot tell you the precise moment when the compass veered off track, but I had a constant dread of what was around the corner next.

I was a middle-aged man with a wealth of experience and yet I was walking around thinking, 'what's next?' Is there anything else negative out there that can hit me next?

Every morning brought a fear of what lay ahead.

The work, football, money, the gambling, the drinking, it was all contriving to pour oil on life's great tapestry.

I got to the stage where I needed help because I knew things were not right.

I was having suicidal thoughts. But did I have any great desire to do anything about them? Not really.

The reason for that was simple.

The reason for that was simple. I was too cowardly.

I have often felt there is a mere hair's breadth between sanity and madness. My situation was becoming progressively worse, but I couldn't see it because I was too busy living in the middle of it all. I was physically, mentally and emotionally spent.

In medical circles they describe it as disambiguation. To you and I what I had has a more common name; a nervous breakdown.

Chapter Twenty

Homeless

TO THOSE who remember my economical playing style, 'sofa-surfing' will sound the perfect way for a man of my years to spend his retirement.

It's a term I use to describe the lost months I spent slumming it in the aftermath of my descent into breakdown.

The reality of my collapse into begging makeshift beds from friends, sons and former drinking friends was, of course, no laughing matter.

In the aftermath of my lapse I had effectively been living in a haphazard fashion for a long time, too long. I was never living rough in the sense of occupying a park bench with an old newspaper and a bottle of Buckfast for company. I always had a roof over my head; it just was not my roof. I was dotting from here to there, trying to find some meaning, some roots in life.

I was down south with some old friends in England where I probably spent around six aimless months.

My son Stephen also put me up, as did my mother and a few old chums and drinking friends in the West of Scotland.

I have known some social animals in my time and when the chips are down these people come forward to help you. They know the score.

No one more so than a fellow who knows me better than most. His name is Bobby McLaughlin, a recovering alcoholic.

Bobby has not had a drink for a long time. I maintain I have never been an alcoholic as such, but I would concede this much; I have had my problems with alcohol.

So Bobby saw the signs with me when I rolled up to spend three weeks living on his couch, the latest in a Cook's Tour of stopping off points.

Concerned by what he was seeing Bobby eventually phoned a gem of a man in Tony Higgins, the former Secretary of the old Scottish Professional Footballers' Association. Tony was a former teammate of mine at Morton and I knew and trusted the man.

Tony came out to Uddingston and left promising to see what he could do. Three days later there were a couple of phone calls and Bobby took me in to see some people in Paisley from the Renfrewshire Council On Addictions (RCA).

Tony wanted me to go to the Priory Clinic in London. Naturally I did not want to go to the Priory in London. Why would I? That's for jumped up celebrities with problems. Then he tried to persuade me to go to the Priory in Glasgow. Again I did not want to go to the Priory in Glasgow. Eventually we settled on a compromise.

As I say, I trusted Tony. The SPFA had helped me once to commemorate the 25th anniversary of me winning the Writers' Footballer of the Year award.

They had organised a tribute evening for me in a little place just off George Square in Glasgow city centre and handed me a few thousand pounds from the proceeds. Which, I should add, I badly needed at that particular time.

I was still married and was still in the family home in Uddingston. But, I will be honest, without that cash they would have repossessed that house. Even then I was living from hand to mouth and the SPFA, through Tony, had done me a favour.

I was assigned a counsellor called Andy Todd, a terrific fella. Another old football friend would also come to my aid in the weeks that followed my referral to the Renfrewshire addictions centre by Tony.

Kenny Hope, the former grade one referee in Scotland, works in that area and I was effectively seconded to his care.

I moved into residential accommodation when they finally took me to Paisley – albeit with a good degree of reluctance on my part.

Looking back now I needed it – badly – but initially I did not want to go.

I went there in a taxi for a consultation with the lady who ran the operation. I felt I had been there two minutes when she broke the news to me that I had been talking for an hour.

She told me I looked awful. That I looked completely and utterly exhausted.

At which point I started to cry, tears rolling down my face as I confirmed her theory. I was exhausted. With life, with my life more specifically.

She wanted to take me in for residential help there and then. But I told her I could not do it – I wanted to go home to my mother's first.

So off I went in a taxi. But I was delaying the inevitable. The next day the taxi came back and in I went again for my own good.

At first it was a question of pride. Where once I was the cock of the north my life was now heading south fast and that was hard to accept.

I had been separated from my wife for a couple of years and I had lost my way.

I finally went in to confront my issues that autumnal day in November 2006 and ended up spending 15 months under the umbrella of the experts in Barrhead.

In March 2008, when I came to the end of the course, I had to move out. For a time I lived in homeless accommodation. With the apron strings of the

RCA cut I had little option but to go and declare myself homeless to the East Renfrewshire Council.

If I said that was easy then I would be lying. As a result of swallowing my pride I spent time in a homeless unit in Barrhead. But I am not ashamed, why should I be? – I am facing up to rebuilding my life.

The truth is this. Had I not changed my lifestyle dramatically by going for help I would not be here to tell this story.

There are no two ways about it. The Good Lord would either have taken me or I would have taken myself.

I would never have the courage for suicide now. But would I have been able to continue as I was back then? No way.

I never ended up with a loaded revolver or a bottle full of tablets. But stepping in front of a train was never the main worry. It was the mental state that made you consider it in the first place.

When you receive a few massive whacks from life's clunking baseball bat then invariably it will take its toll. Mentally and physically. And it did on me.

Now I feel as if life is returning to an even keel and much of that is down to my old Morton teammate and union chum Tony.

He is a good guy. No, let me put it stronger than that, he is a really fucking good guy.

He is a big jovial type of character who is quick-witted and is a very smart man. He is absolutely nobody's fool when it comes to looking after his life.

He is an educated man, but a down to earth man. A fella who knows what the game of football and its protagonists are all about. He knows what makes us ex-pros tick and what the game can do both for people and to them when it's all over.

He was unbelievably helpful to me when I needed it most and I will never forget that.

Tony now has a big job with FIFPRO and has moved beyond Scotland's modest borders. But he has always kept in contact with what I have been doing with the RCA.

He tried to set up similar situations with some other ex-pros falling on harder times. Ian Wallace was once a £1 million striker with Nottingham Forest and a Scotland international – but like me he found the going tough after he stopped playing. Sadly, Ian did not go through the system like I did.

Tony looked after me because I like to think he is a friend of mine.

He always will be. I might not always be the best of friends to him, but he will always be regarded by me as one of my best pals.

I played with Tony at Cappielow and I can confidently say we were the fattest forward line in the Premier League.

When we played up front together there were only two of us, but side-by-side we were the equivalent of a three man forward line. We were formidable – in girth at least.

We played together and we socialised together. Tony would be the first guy to let you know he liked a bottle of beer – but he knew where to stop.

Tony had a year of playing with George Best at Hibs later in his career.

The late Manchester United and Northern Ireland legend had a brief spell at Easter Road in 1979 when the old chairman there, Tom Hart, agreed to pay him £2,000 a game. This was at a time when I was Player of the Year and earning less than a 10th of that.

People in glass houses should always put down the stone and walk away, but George was overweight and bloated by the time he rolled up in Edinburgh, though he brought in the crowds wherever he went. I was sorry to hear of his death a few years ago.

But Tony uses a great line on the after dinner speaking circuit, where he is an entertaining performer, saying that the year he spent with George Best at Hibs was the equivalent of spending a fortnight with Andy Ritchie at Morton...

I think he means it in a kind of nice way. I am taking it like that anyway.

Tony would also like to have helped Mike Galloway, a former Hearts, Celtic and Scotland midfielder who came close to death following a horrific car crash at Portsmouth.

For whatever reason that did not work out either, but I did the course and now it is time for me to move on. I cannot afford to concern myself with others. And I can never be complacent.

My problems have not disappeared because I sought some help. They never go away. I have to make a life of my own again now.

It is a constant battle for me to stay ahead of the game and not go backwards mentally. For that to be the case I must always accept the help of others.

But Tony did a big thing for me at a time when I really needed it and the people at RCA have been great.

I still keep in touch with Andy, my counsellor there. He's a pal now as much as anything. You cannot lay yourself bare to other people like that and not make friends along the way.

He knows my life inside out because we spent every day he worked in situations where we did nothing else but talk about my problems. Numerous as they were.

I do not know that we ever actually solved anything as such. We never put anything truly to bed. You do not wave a magic wand and make deep-rooted issues go away. But you can gain some kind of insight into them, a new way of thinking and that is all you can ask.

So I made friends there and I found shelter when I needed it.

But you cannot hide yourself away forever. You cannot cocoon yourself into a shell.

It is now the time to get back into the big wide world and see what is going on. Hopefully with different attitudes and a new outlook.

There are still loose ends to be tied up. Doing this and getting my story down in print – as a warning to others as much as a therapy for me – is just one of those.

I could have lost my life at one time. I am proud to say after all these years that I am still here.

Chapter Twenty-one

Do They Mean Me?

THE OLDER I get the more I realise that a man can be a hostage to his own image. And I am damned if I can do anything to change mine.

People will speak to me, talk to me and address me in a certain manner and, to this day, I still feel they must be talking about someone else.

It's a very strange thing. To have complete strangers coming up and telling you how something you did 30 years ago affected them personally.

Invariably I do not know these people from Adam. It has happened many times through conversations with fathers, grandfathers or whoever. They were told something or think they saw something or were reminded of something. More often than not, to me, it's a misconceived idea and a distortion of reality.

The impression some folk have is of a guy who used to fly down to Greenock without a plane, step into the phone box on the main road at Cappielow and change myself into a blue and white striped Superman outfit. I would step on the pitch, do nothing but ping a couple of 30 yarders into the top corner, produce a cigar then head straight back up the road again.

People have this soft focus sepia-tinged image of me out of keeping with reality. Or, as I prefer to call it, an image of me, which has two coats of white paint lathered on top. It can be very flattering when people come up to you and say nice things. When they tell you the impact you had on their life.

But, deep down in my head I am always thinking the same thing. I am catching their eye, I am maintaining contact, I am talking and bantering and I am laughing and joking. But so far as I am concerned the man they are talking about is not really me.

My mother has always been an inherently wise woman. She is never far off the money with her observations on life.

And what she always says is that, despite the image, I am basically a shy person. Deep down I feel that way about things. I am not naturally a gregarious person. But the perception I have is that people think I am the very opposite.

Maybe that's my fault. Of course it is my fault. I have spent my whole life cutting around like a performing monkey.

That I have been able to do that has owed much to alcohol and substances. Those got me through some very awkward social circumstances in my time.

Not least when the whole country wanted a slice of me in my Player of the Year season.

The only place I felt really comfortable, the only place where I felt I was being completely myself, was on the park.

When I felt good and I was fit and active that was the only place where I felt really at ease.

Don't get me wrong. It is not as if people have been slating me and getting the wrong idea; most of the stuff I have read about myself down the years has been positive and to my benefit; affectionate even.

They coined phrases to describe me; the Idle Idol, the Ambling Alp. Not uncomplimentary exactly, but not terms of wholesome praise either.

I can remember people saying of me in my early days that I was of a similar ilk to George Connelly, my enigmatic former Celtic teammate and another who quit the game too early. And when they said that I tended to think; 'well if I have half the talent of that guy I'll take that'.

But the fact is that I started to develop the persona that whatever people wanted me to be I would be.

If folk wanted me to be a nice guy I would be that man. If I was expected to be loud and obnoxious I could be good at that as well. One-line quips? No problem. So I was performing for whatever audience I found myself in.

At heart I like to think I am a nice guy. But sometimes people misconstrued niceness in me for softness.

But in one way I am certainly trying to be more assertive now. I do not do things I don't want to do now. I do not perform any longer. Either on or off the pitch.

I do not mean that literally, obviously. There are always things in life you simply have to do. But I am a lot more selective in what I will do now, I do not feel pressure to do anything now.

I'm a lot calmer in my life in general. But basically if you stripped away all the coats and veneers I believe I am basically a shy person. It would never be in my nature to build myself up or put myself forward.

Neither would I necessarily see other football players and think, 'he's a chip off the old block'.

Folk called me up and tried to make comparisons between me and the likes of Alexei Eremenko, who played for Kilmarnock for a season. Or even Kris Boyd in his Rangers days.

But I do not buy any of them. There is only one guy I ever really thought had a similar thing going on to me.

I remember reading an article on Alan Ball at Southampton. He stopped the training and told the players, 'either do this or it is back to the running track. Every five passes I want Matt Le Tissier to touch the ball.'

I remember thinking that was how Benny wanted it at Morton. 'Get the ball to Andy,' was always the cry.

Le Tissier is the only example I can think of where a player has even vaguely reminded me of myself.

I remember being chief scout at Celtic and I went to Loftus Road to see him play for the England B team. He was magnificent.

He also scored the best goal I have ever seen in my life live at a football game in a friendly between Southampton and Kilmarnock, not long after Tommy Burns took over as manager at Rugby Park.

He started in his own half; beat three or four people cut inside and plonked it in the top corner from 30 yards.

It was pre-season and there would have been no more than 1,000 people there. I was on my feet in raptures at this goal despite sitting in the director's box where that kind of thing is frowned upon. I was the only one standing and I can still see that goal in my mind's eye.

It was magic and I could feel all the blood rushing to my head. I was clapping like an idiot. It was just that spark of genius I could appreciate and at that time he was scoring those kinds of goals every week on the telly.

At the risk of sounding arrogant he was similar to myself. He was comfortable at an unfashionable club, he played all his best football at Southampton and he would have been two steps behind everyone else in a race. But he would be five steps ahead of them in his head.

I remember Stan Bowles being a bit like that at Queen's Park Rangers as well. They were mavericks and so was I.

Whenever we were struggling at Morton I would hear Benny barking from the dug-out, 'get the ball to him, get the ball to Andy'.

Big Jock Stein would say the same of wee Jimmy Johnstone as well. 'Go on, on you go.'

I was happy to take the ball whenever. Sometimes if they gave me the wrong ball I would give them it straight back again the same way. But I never hid from possession.

The bravest players when I played football were the guys who played up front.

In that era defenders went right through you saying, 'fuck it', and kicked you right up the rear end.

I remember playing in my only Old Firm game for Celtic against Rangers at Ibrox and big Tam Forsyth came right through the back of me. He hammered me from behind so hard that I could feel the roots of my teeth shaking.

I made to get up and as I did it John Greig ran past and stood on my hand with his big aluminium studs. I can still hear the crunch in a quiet room. He broke two bones in my hand. It was that kind of game back then.

Towards the 1980s things began to change. Charlie Nicholas and George McCluskey at Celtic and wee John McDonald at Rangers were getting it nowhere near as bad.

You always got your first tackle for nothing. No booking, no talking to. So you were told to make it count.

Guys like the late Davie Cooper at Rangers and Davie Provan at Celtic would be the prime targets.

The managers would say, 'you'll get one for fuck all until you're booked, so make sure you give it to him sore.'

You often hear players now saying they went in hard but never meant to hurt the guy. Back in the 1970s there was no ambiguity. If the player was not hurt there would be a manager standing waiting in the dressing room at half-time dying to know why.

If you were the one being carted off on that stretcher with a leg dangling over the side and hanging by a thread, they were quite happy. It was job done.

There was no room for misconstruing intentions. There was none of this namby pamby, pretend nonsense of trying to win the ball. Everyone knew the score.

My hardest opponents were a bit more intelligent than that. They had a bit more about them and did not need to stretch the laws of the game to succeed.

Paul Hegarty at Dundee United was probably the toughest centre-half I faced. He was very, very hard to get the better of.

He was very good in the air and could cover the ground, but he was not the biggest. He was physically strong, read the game well and had a good partner in David Narey. He was a thinking man's centre-half with good instincts and I always had a lot of problems with him.

I still scored goals against Dundee United. But Paul was the closest you could have got then to what we call a modern day centre-half. He was a bit more sophisticated than the rest and could assess situations.

He had started his career as a centre-forward, which probably helped. Willie Miller at Aberdeen, another tough opponent, was the same.

In Hegarty and Narey and Miller and Alex McLeish at Aberdeen I came up against two of the best defensive partnerships Scottish football had seen.

Before Miller and McLeish formed a formidable pairing I played up at Aberdeen one night against Willie and his previous partner Willie Young.

I was a 16 and a half-year-old boy at the time and Willie Young was Scotland's central-defender at the time and just six months away from joining Arsenal. I scored the winning goal in a 2–1 League Cup win.

It's fair to say Miller was one of my harder opponents as well, although I always seemed to excel against Aberdeen. I gave Dundee United a heluva time of it as well, if truth be told.

That was my job. You accepted you were up against good players and you wanted them to think you were a good player as well. I wanted these guys to see what I could do.

No one more so than George Best, a man who made my antics seem like almost saintly in comparison.

Best had come up to Scotland for £2,000 a game at the invitation of the Hibs chairman Tom Hart.

He was a pale shadow of the European Cup winning, snake-hipped legend of his heyday. But he was still George fucking Best and here he was coming to play Morton at Cappielow a couple of weeks before Christmas in 1979.

Of course, in my mind, he was not coming to play Morton. He was coming to play me.

I just wanted him to know who I was. He had played against the best players in the world; he had BEEN the best player in the world.

And now he was coming down to Greenock that day to play against me. And the papers were full of it; Best the old master against Ritchie, the young pretender.

I don't know why I was so determined to do well against him. I can only compare it to the X-Factor when guys go on because they want to sing on the same stage as Robbie Williams. These guys want Robbie Williams to say they are a great singer.

What I desperately wanted was for George Best to say I was a great football player. I was so ready to do it and show the tricks and skills and show what I had and beat Hibs that day. In the event he failed to show up because he had gone on the drink again and I felt so disappointed. I was deflated, totally flat because it denied me the opportunity to do my stuff.

The chance to prove beyond all reasonable doubt that Scottish football had never seen my likes. And, I regret to say without a hint of arrogance or bombast, probably never will again.

Chapter Twenty-two

The Ba's Burst

Maybe it's my age. Maybe I am a lost cause. I try, I really do try to be as open-minded about Scottish football as I can possibly be.

But the truth is this. I watch the modern day Scottish game and then I look back into the recesses of my own memory and I come to an inescapable conclusion. Football in this country was better in my day than it is now and the reason for that is simple; the players were better.

There's no question Scottish football is now faster than it used to be and the players are fitter, bigger and stronger. But technically and mentally the players I played with were superior to the current crop and I would argue that with anyone who cared to challenge me.

You could go to Partick Thistle or go to Morton or any of the less fashionable clubs 20 to 30 years ago and know there would be two or three genuinely good players there.

I know what they say; that ex-players never ever had a bad game. I will tell anyone who will listen that I cannot remember ever having one.

It is easy to sit and quibble. And I am sure Craig Levein or Mark Wotte, the SFA technical director, would tell you all about initiatives going on behind the scenes. So I do try to be open-minded and objective about it. But as my girlfriend might say, the older I get the harder it is to get me excited.

It is not only Scotland where the standard is poor. People have this idea that the English Premiership is full of great football. And sometimes it is. But from what I see the greatest favour television does the Premiership is to edit it carefully. Because some of the games I watch would have no one off their feet.

But even in comparison with the English League Scottish football is in a bad way. I will go along and watch it as an SPL delegate and try to see the positives. But there was one day at the end of last year when it was summed up for me when I went from watching the ridiculous to watching the sublime.

There was a game at Easter Road, Edinburgh between Hibernian and Rangers and I was in the house with a remote control in one hand and a mug of tea in the other. Spain's El Classico between Real Madrid and Barcelona was also on Sky later the same night. It was something to relish.

But it is impossible to say just how bad the Scottish game was. The first half was appalling.

The Spanish game? It was like watching a different sport. There were players who could actually control, caress and pass the ball.

The players seemed to have an awareness of what was happening around them. They had a mentality whereby they wanted to play the game the right way. There were combination plays, one-touch movements, excellent control. It was not just a different league or a different sport. It was a different planet.

I always say that 60 per cent of football is played in your head, the rest with your feet. I like watching players who can pass the ball, raise their head and change the pattern of a whole game. But there is very little of that in the SPL these days.

People will ask if we ever had players like that? In response I think we did, without question.

You could have gone to Partick Thistle a few years ago and, okay, Chic Charnley could not run as fast as everybody else. But he could certainly control the ball and pass it. And he had a vision and awareness. The good players have that because they can play the game in their heads.

It would be wrong to spread the impression that everyone was Pele when I was growing up. The passing years make everyone seem better than they really were. Me included.

It's a misconception in Greenock that people only came to Morton games to cheer me.

I thought I could play, but I had plenty of critics as well and it was my job to prove these people wrong just like it is the job of the current players to do the same to me.

I might be out of order here, but it did seem as if we had more good players and the evidence and achievements backed that up. It is indisputable.

Celtic reached two European Cup Finals, winning one, with a team of Scots drawn from within 30 miles of Glasgow.

Rangers lost the Cup Winners' Cup Final of 1967, but won it in 1972. Again with a team of Scots and no overseas players. Dundee, Hibs, Kilmarnock and Dunfermline all reached the latter stages of European competitions while the 'New Firm' of Aberdeen and Dundee United dominated the 1980s, the Dons becoming only the third side to win a European trophy.

People watched those teams in good numbers and went off after the game to talk about players over a pint down the pub. Or went home and talked about them there. Now? The last thing anyone talks about these days is the players.

Listen to a radio phone-in now and it'll be subjects, which have nothing to do with players or even football being talked to death. Or some poor referee will be getting it in the neck as half the country tries to find out what school he went to. It is a depressing scenario.

When I was growing up I had my heroes, guys I believed could play the game as it should be played.

My dad would take me and my brother to Motherwell games. Liam was only ever interested in sweets and the badges he could get, but I was more interested in the football. There were players like Willie Hunter and Pat Quinn and Ian St John.

They were my early introduction to football. Going back into the mists of time there were players only Motherwell people would have heard of like Charlie Aitken or Jumbo Muir.

And very early on there was a guy from my hometown of Bellshill who played in the team. His name was Bobby McCallum, a left full-back who played for Scotland. He was a fantastic left-back, he would have been the perfect modern day overlapping full-back. He had a left foot, which could curl a tennis ball into a tin can from 30 yards.

The problem with Bobby was one typical of many Scottish players. It was always a good night in the Orb in Bellshill on a Friday night and rumour had it that Bobby enjoyed them more than most. They always said that how he played on a Saturday was generally dictated by whether he had gone to bed the night before.

But anyone will tell you he should have been a star with bigger clubs. And every team in Scotland had a Bobby McCallum at that time. Maybe even two or three of them.

Tommy McLean, for example, was a young player at Kilmarnock before moving to Rangers, while Ross Mathie was a terrific Rugby Park centre-forward. You also had Donald Ford at Hearts scoring goals and others throughout the League. It was the rule, not the exception. There were heroes and role models to copy at every club and in every town in Scotland.

When I was young I went onto the ground staff at Celtic and I would go along to training in the morning and watched the guys who had won the European Cup.

What a player Bobby Murdoch was. Bobby Lennox, Billy McNeill and Jimmy Johnstone were still there as well and I was lucky enough to play with guys like those as a young reserve player.

They were coming to the end of their careers but they had so much to pass down. They led by example. On the field as well as off it. They were good guys; they took time out to teach the young players. Who is good enough to have anything worth passing on now? Who do players learn their tricks from now?

I learned my football in the Celtic reserves and had it relatively easy. At 16 years of age I was called back from the juniors at Rob Roy and went straight into the Celtic reserve team with the likes of wee Jinky, Harry Hood, George Connelly and Tommy Callaghan. We were talking absolute top drawer, quality football players. Put simply, they were able to play the game.

They did not waste their time telling young players to get into the gymnasium to build themselves up or spend their days telling us what to eat or when to sleep.

By the time I got to 18 I was discovering Smirnoff and sex and those guys would tell you all you needed to know about that. But they did not waste their time telling you how to play football; that was done out on the big green patch of grass.

They did not come along to training and tell you not to do this or to do that. They did not advise you to get yourself a good agent.

All they told you was all any footballer needs to know. 'You are coming out to play football with us and if I am giving you the ball the right way I want you to give it back to me in the same fashion.' There was no shit about systems or tactics or sports science. It was not rocket science. You simply had to be able to play football and do the right things on the pitch.

Big Jock Stein's assistant Sean Fallon or the reserve coach Willie Fernie did not have to make the decision about whether I was ready for the reserves at 16. They just had to ask the older players, because they knew.

If a boy was out of his depth they could smell it. They also knew when a young player would have no problems because, as I say, the game is played in the head. You had to produce for the guys you were playing with as much as you did for the manager. If you did not you didn't get a game, simple. The old pros decided who the good players were and I was lucky enough to be able to go and play with them at 16 and a half.

I remember playing in my first reserve game, a 5–4 win over Partick Thistle at Celtic Park. It was a great game with great players and that was where you learned your trade. Not on a Largs course or on a blackboard. It was there; there on that pitch.

It follows as sure as night follows day, then, that if the football being played now is poor and technically deficient then the modern day player is not learning properly. And right now that is how it looks to me.

I do not claim to have any deep-rooted theories on where it all went wrong or how to fix it. I wish I did.

I lived through the 60s, 70s, 80s and 90s, but I cannot point to a date and say, 'that's when it all started going wrong'.

All I know is what I see and I still adopt the same ethos as to how the game should be played as I did in the early 70s.

Show me someone playing fitba and I will tell you if they can play or not. I will tell you if they are good enough. Because to me you either have it or you do not. It is nature, not nurture.

There are players who have improved and made the best of themselves certainly. But you must have that basic ability to be a real player.

No one was telling me from seven years of age how to be a football player. I think that kills the joy of football for a lot of kids now. It is all structured and regimented and about not making mistakes.

I remember going to watch kids' games involving wee boys whose voices had not broken yet.

And the coaches would be cursing and swearing at them and talking to them in footballing terms which make no sense. If I did not understand them how the hell could a 10-year-old get it?

They bring them in now at eight and nine and coach the football out of them. They take the joy away.

Personally I would always want to treat young footballers the way I treated my own two sons.

But I was lucky enough to get a coaching job at Celtic Park when Tommy Burns took me back and I eventually had to hold up my hands and say I was not a good coach of kids because I did not have the patience.

The best people in my early years in football were patient, patient people. Willie Fernie was a soft, kind man who told you what you needed to know at that moment in time. I watch kids' football now and I'm not sure a lot of the people teaching them are much better than I was.

It's all about kits and academies and initiatives now. Me? I learned about football playing with my pals in the street. These days parents are terrified to let their boys cross the door. Street football is dead thanks to the society we live in now.

Kids do not want to play football now unless it is regimented and organised for them.

The first night I went to coach the kids at Celtic I turned up at the old Helenvale Complex and I was stunned to see a stream of big 4x4s and big Volvos turning up, the boys all leaping out with all the kit and gear.

It set me to thinking about getting the green Number 35 bus from Bellshill into Parkhead Cross and feeling the fear because I was a country bumpkin heading for the big town.

I remember thinking I was getting in above my head and worrying I was not good enough to be there. I would walk from the bus stop to the Barrowfield training pitches with a knot in my stomach.

It used to be at Celtic that only the best got a crack at it. There were not a lot of us.

This night at Helenvale it was like the cast of Braveheart coming over the hill, hundreds of kids rolling up with all the latest stuff. And I remember thinking, 'what we going to do with all these kids?'

Big Jock used to tell his coaches to bring him only the very best. He did not want to be a great servant of the community; he wanted to be a great manager of Celtic. A good coach can make a good player better, but the same coach will not make a bad player good.

As a youth coach at St Mirren I worked with the manager Jimmy Bone and we had great discussions about the game, great arguments as well.

I remember him telling me he was planning to take a young player for double training sessions and do this and that with him to make the lad better. He wanted me to try this and fix that to help as well.

Maybe I was wrong, but I told him straight. 'Jimmy, you are wasting your fucking time.'

'What do you mean?' he asked. 'It's our job to do it, to make him better.'

'Maybe so Jimmy,' I responded. 'But he can't fucking play! He runs about, he make tackles, he clatters in and gets about the ball. But the basics aren't there. He can't play.'

As I said in fairly forceful terms, I could not make honey out of manure. I could not wrap tinsel around a lifeless tree.

Maybe Jimmy was more professional than me, maybe he was just more optimistic. But either way we ended up shouting and bawling at each other.

Maybe it's one of the reasons my managerial career was short-lived, I do not know. But it seems to me that no one has a handle on how to fix things right now, there's no leadership.

In my role as an SPL delegate I said something to a high profile manager one day, which made him throw his head back in laughter.

I said to him, 'I know what you guys are doing. You are doing what we have all done in this game; you are winging it. You do not have a clue what you are going to do next.'

He laughed because he knew I was right. The manager in question was a smart guy, a man who knows what people want to hear and plays the media game brilliantly. But he has no more idea about how to fix Scottish football than the rest of us.

There are managers, guys who have been good pals of mine, who suddenly get that job and start making out like they are the keepers of the game's secrets. They talk as if they are reinventing the wheel; they are not. Neither are they splitting the atom. It is a simple game, but you would never think it to hear them.

Too much information is worse than none at all. I always remember the day Jock Stein read out my name for the first time for the Celtic first team.

We were playing Dundee United and as he ran through everything, I turned to a teammate, Jim Brogan.

'Did he just read my name out there?' I asked.

'Aye, you're playing,' says Jim.

I knew Brogan was a bit of a character, so I still was not sure. But I was too afraid to ask big Jock.

All the other players got up to get ready, but I kept sitting because I had not actually heard my name being read out. I finally managed to confirm that I would indeed by playing number seven that day.

But it never came from Jock. Ten minutes before the game the referee came in and the clacking of studs was getting louder in the dressing room. And he still had not said anything to me about how to approach my first-team debut for Celtic, not a word.

My brain was like mashed potatoes and I started to panic a bit because I was out my comfort zone. Had he said to me 'just take your kit off and put your coat back on, I was only kidding,' I would have been delighted.

I had a feeling of absolute fucking terror. As if I had never played the game before.

Eventually he tapped me on the back and said, 'on you go, play on the right-hand side and give the ball to other players and look after it. Do the things you do all the time.'

And that was it. From the greatest man ever to manage Celtic Football Club. Simple, straightforward advice.

These days we coach kids to death from the age of seven and eight. Great, that is nice. But is all the coaching actually improving anything? I do not think so.

The cult of the manager has grown in recent times and because of that the balance is out of kilter. People do not talk so much about players now.

I always remember taking an absolute hounding from the manager and assistant manager at Morton one day for something or other before I snapped.

'Listen, the only criticism I give a fuck about is the criticism I get from the other players.'

Benny Rooney went bananas at that, but it was true. Only your teammates could dig you out a hole.

In those days there was never the barrage of nonsense you witness from technical areas these days, with pointing and elaborate hand gestures every 10 seconds.

I never looked at the dugout. Never. These days players are constantly looking all the time because they have no independence of thought.

If they have a shot at goal and it does not go in they look at the dugout. And the manager will be ranting and raving at them over a relative triviality they can do nothing about. That's a fairly new thing.

If big Jock Stein started to roar out the dugout at Celtic you knew you were in serious, serious trouble.

I never looked to the dugout for inspiration because I failed to see what they could possibly do to help me. The guys by my side or behind me could help me because they could lay on a chance for me to score the next time.

But all this nonsense you see now is like a *Day at The Races* with the Marx Brothers. Or like watching John McCrirrick on *Channel Four Racing*.

As I said to my SPL manager pal, a lot of these guys are winging it.

Maybe I have a cheek to talk because I did not do much managing, but to me a coach is there to sign good players, get teams organised and win games. As I see it systems and tactics are simple; it is all about making sure you do not put round pegs in square holes.

You talk to kids now who leave teams because they are right-wingers and they cannot get in the team.

When I hear that I'll say to them, 'why don't you go and play on the left-wing then?' And all you get back is, 'no I'm a right-winger.'

That's another of the ways in which the Scottish game has changed. Too many players are desperate to pigeonhole themselves in a set position instead of learning what they should be learning; to be good all round footballers.

I used to take a game of football wherever I could get one. It did not matter if I was centre-half because I was taller than some. Or if I played right-midfield. Or as a forward, as I finished up.

Not everything has gone backwards. When I stand in tunnels these days as a match delegate I see players who look bigger, fitter and stronger than they ever were. That is progress.

I was a small, fat boy at 14 – and some said a big fat boy at 25. And when I became a football player a gymnasium was a form of punishment. The modern day player eats pasta. We did not, we ate a big steak. I did not like steaks much, but I ate them just the same.

Maybe because players do not eat steaks any longer the Scottish game is quicker now and the movement is faster. Five times quicker probably. But to me it's 10 times slower in the mind.

I know the times change. I am no Luddite.

You see Old Firm players now coming out of dressing rooms with these big headphones on not looking at anybody and carrying a bag full of aftershaves and perfumes, which cost half the Greek national debt.

Their salaries are enormous and they portray an image of arrogance. That is nothing new. There was a lot of arrogance among very good football players when I played as well. I was probably guilty on that score myself.

But I never earned a fraction of what these guys earn now. And some folk might say I had more right to than these fellas. Right now they are just not good enough and results in Europe prove it.

Is there a way back for the Scottish game? Only if we find a way to get some better players.

We had good players, but we do not now. As I say, I cannot say with any certainty when that began to happen.

December 15 1995 would be as good a guess as any, because that is the day the Bosman ruling allowing players unrestricted freedom of movement came in. For Scottish football, if not the players, that has been a disaster.

Had the Bosman rule been around when I was a player I would have had a year, maybe two, at Morton then I would have been gone. That is the truth.

I scored 30 goals a season when I went there. So my departure on freedom of contract might have been bad for Morton, but financially it would have done me the power of good.

I thought when I went to Cappielow I was taking two steps back to take three steps forward.

And I produced the goods, I scored goals. But because I was under contract and Hal Stewart wanted £1 million for me I could never leave. Players were slaves to the club and I was the last slave left when others were manning the life rafts and bailing out.

I spoke to Tony Higgins, the players' union man and my former teammate, about this once and I remember saying I could never have imagined what it would be like when Bosman came in. If I am honest I would only ever have signed for a year at any club had we had the freedom back then.

I have a low boredom threshold at the best of times so having the freedom to move around regularly would have been great for me.

Jackie Charlton tried to sign me for Sheffield Wednesday and I was so desperate to go to England. Allan Mullery tried to sign me for Brighton as well and I could well visualise myself playing down there and living on the south coast. They had just sold Peter Ward to Nottingham Forest for £1 million and wanted me as his replacement. But Morton played hardball.

Ironically Brighton did sign Andy Ritchie as part of the deal – but it was the Andy Ritchie who played for Manchester United, not me. Once again, I had been jilted at the altar.

So Bosman has been a liberating force for players, but it has been shocking for the Scottish game in general.

I'm not just talking about the top of the tree either, I mean all the way down the food chain.

The game is different, but you would be hard pressed to say it is better. Now clubs rely on sponsors, broadcasters and sugar daddies buying clubs to use them as play toys.

There was a time in Scottish football when the likes of Hal Stewart or Jack Steedman at Clydebank sold a player a year to keep afloat. But they did more than that, they sold football. They sold dreams to players. And they sold hope and glory to supporters.

Now that job has fallen to Sky, radio and television and newspapers to do that. Football clubs, by and large, treat customers like chewing gum stuck to their shoes. They do not understand the importance of selling the game.

Where we go from here is anyone's guess. For my money the best player Scottish football has seen in recent times was Henrik Larsson.

Henrik was a top, top player and he was well paid and liked scoring goals for Celtic.

But it was no great surprise to me at the end of his Celtic career that he went on to win medals with Manchester United and Barcelona, playing with the best players in the world.

That was testimony to how good Larsson was. Suddenly people were accepting he genuinely was a good player; he was not just running past static Scottish defenders.

He was a real top quality football player and a throwback to the 1970s when we had some of the best players in Europe in our League.

Sadly we have no Henrik Larssons now. No Brian Laudrups and no Paul Gascoignes. Nor, for that matter, an Andy Ritchie. And all the refereeing debates and off field rows in the world can't hide that.

Chapter Twenty-three

And so the Story Ends

I HAVE PRECIOUS few dreams in life left. Those I still harbour are relatively modest.

All I hope is that the coming years are a trifle better than those that preceded them. As I say, my ambitions are grounded.

There is plenty I want in my life. But there is no longer much which drags me from bed in the morning with a mission to achieve.

I have come through some dark times in the last five years. My physical strength is good again, back where I want it to be. I cannot say the same of my mental health. That's an open secret by now.

What I can say is this; my treatment is working. I have learned to separate my needs from my wants.

Let me explain. My wants were always greater than my needs. If I had a big car I wanted a bigger one. I can step away from that now. I can find satisfaction in simpler pleasures these days.

To say I am content would be putting it strongly. To say I am surviving would be more accurate.

For me to feel comfortable in my current mode of survival is, in itself, a kind of triumph. Because, heaven knows, I do not have much.

But, as the tragic death of Gary Speed demonstrates, possessions are no guarantee of happiness. There was a man who had a lovely wife, two sons, a decorated career, international recognition, the looks of a model and was never off the TV. There seem to have been words with his wife, but to me there was no rhyme or reason to that man's suicide. There rarely is to any suicide.

To me there is a hair's breadth between being in control of your sanity and being totally and completely insane.

I have gone right to the edge a couple of times. Maybe more than a couple of times.

I have climbed from bed with heavy limbs of a morning and thought to myself, 'life is dealing me from the bottom of the pack here'. It affected me in some odd ways.

I remember at one stage giving things away; all my possessions. People I know still talk about it. I would give my watch away on impulse purely because I was unwell. Nothing had any value to me.

I did it for one reason; I was ill. My possessions had no great value and neither did my life as a whole.

And yet the truth is this. Just as I felt life was treating me badly so I also remember when life was treating me very well indeed. And even then I didn't feel so good.

When I had money I was unhappy. And when I did not? You can finish the sentence by now. Suffice to say the grass was always greener.

Many people, medical people, have asked me if I ever contemplated suicide. I told them I had not.

I always swatted it aside by saying I was too much of a coward. But when you see and hear things like Gary Speed you realise that you do not really need to be a coward to do that. On the contrary, you need to be a very brave man. Very brave indeed.

Alternatively you need to have crossed the hair's breadth line I spoke about. The one that has carried me right to the brink more than once. The one from which I am grateful to say I have pulled back.

I have felt bad in my life. I have felt bad for prolonged periods. But, thankfully, I was never that brave.

I stayed the right side of the line and I know one thing. My salvation was being able to go and talk to people; good people who knew how to lead a man to land.

Maybe I've just been lucky that, at critical junctures of my life, I have had those people to talk to. Be it close friends or family. Or the professional help I had when I really needed it.

I like to think I have been fortunate. I have been the right man, in the right place at the right time.

I did not get everything right in my football career and my life in general. And that is an understatement.

But when it mattered most I pulled back from the brink. And for that alone I feel grateful, proud and more than a little humble.

Life has not always been a picnic. But my little granddaughter is growing up and seeing that makes every minute feel like a blessing. A small blessing, but a very welcome one.